AAT

Qualifications and Credit Framework (QCF)

AQ2013
LEVEL 3 DIPLOMA IN ACCOUNTING

(QCF)

QUESTION BANK

Costs and Revenues

2015 Edition

For assessments from September 2015

Third edition June 2015
ISBN 9781 4727 2202 7

Previous edition June 2014
ISBN 9781 4727 0936 3

British Library Cataloguing-in-Publication Data
A catalogue record for this book is available from the British Library

Published by
BPP Learning Media Ltd
BPP House
Aldine Place
London W12 8AA

www.bpp.com/learningmedia

Printed in the United Kingdom by Martins of Berwick
Sea View Works
Spittal
Berwick-Upon-Tweed
TD15 1RS

CONTENTS

A NOTE ABOUT COPYRIGHT

Dear Customer

What does the little © mean and why does it matter?

Your market-leading BPP books, course materials and e-learning materials do not write and update themselves. People write them on their own behalf or as employees of an organisation that invests in this activity. Copyright law protects their livelihoods. It does so by creating rights over the use of the content.

Breach of copyright is a form of theft – as well being a criminal offence in some jurisdictions, it is potentially a serious breach of professional ethics.

With current technology, things might seem a bit hazy but, basically, without the express permission of BPP Learning Media:

- Photocopying our materials is a breach of copyright

- Scanning, ripcasting or conversion of our digital materials into different file formats, uploading them to Facebook or emailing them to your friends is a breach of copyright

You can, of course, sell your books, in the form in which you have bought them – once you have finished with them. (Is this fair to your fellow students? We update for a reason). Please note the e-products are sold on a single user licence basis: we do not supply 'unlock' codes to people who have bought them secondhand.

And what about outside the UK? BPP Learning Media strives to make our materials available at prices students can afford by local printing arrangements, pricing policies and partnerships which are clearly listed on our website. A tiny minority ignore this and indulge in criminal activity by illegally photocopying our material or supporting organisations that do. If they act illegally and unethically in one area, can you really trust them?

INTRODUCTION

This is BPP Learning Media's AAT Question Bank for Costs and Revenues. It is part of a suite of ground-breaking resources produced by BPP Learning Media for the AAT's assessments under the Qualification and Credit Framework.

The Costs and Revenues assessment will be **computer assessed**. As well as being available in the traditional paper format, this **Question Bank is available in an online environment** containing tasks similar to those you will encounter in the AAT's testing environment. BPP Learning Media believe that the best way to practise for an online assessment is in an online environment. However, if you are unable to practise in the online environment you will find that all tasks in the paper Question Bank have been written in a style that is as close as possible to the style that you will be presented with in your online assessment.

This Question Bank has been written in conjunction with the BPP Text, and has been carefully designed to enable students to practise all of the learning outcomes and assessment criteria for the units that make up Costs and Revenues. It is fully up to date as at June 2015 and reflects both the AAT's unit guide and the sample assessment provided by the AAT.

This Question Bank contains these key features:

- Tasks corresponding to each chapter of the Text. Some tasks are designed for learning purposes, others are of assessment standard

- The AAT's AQ2013 sample assessments and answers for Costs and Revenues and further BPP practice assessments

The emphasis in all tasks and assessments is on the practical application of the skills acquired.

VAT

You may find tasks throughout this Question Bank that need you to calculate or be aware of a rate of VAT. This is stated at 20% in these examples and questions.

Approaching the assessment

When you sit the assessment it is very important that you follow the on screen instructions. This means you need to carefully read the instructions, both on the introduction screens and during specific tasks.

When you access the assessment you should be presented with an introductory screen with information similar to that shown below (taken from the introductory screen from the AAT's AQ2013 Sample Assessment for Costs and Revenues).

We have provided the following assessment to help you familiarise yourself with AAT's e-assessment environment. It is designed to demonstrate as many as possible of the question types you may find in a live assessment. It is not designed to be used on its own to determine whether you are ready for a live assessment.

This assessment contains <u>10 tasks</u> and you should attempt and aim to complete EVERY task.
Each task is independent. You will not need to refer to your answers to previous tasks.
Read every task carefully to make sure you understand what is required.

Where the date is relevant, it is given in the task data.
Both minus signs and brackets can be used to indicate negative numbers UNLESS task instructions say otherwise.

You must use a full stop to indicate a decimal point.
For example, write 100.57 NOT 100,57 or 100 57

You may use a comma to indicate a number in the thousands, but you don't have to.
For example, 10000 and 10,000 are both OK.

Other indicators are not compatible with the computer-marked system.

The actual instructions will vary depending on the subject you are studying for. It is very important you read the instructions on the introductory screen and apply them in the assessment. You don't want to lose marks when you know the correct answer just because you have not entered it in the right format.

In general, the rules set out in the AAT Sample Assessments for the subject you are studying for will apply in the real assessment, but you should again read the information on this screen in the real assessment carefully just to make sure. This screen may also confirm the VAT rate used if applicable.

A full stop is needed to indicate a decimal point. We would recommend using minus signs to indicate negative numbers and leaving out the comma signs to indicate thousands, as this results in a lower number of key strokes and less margin for error when working under time pressure. Having said that, you can use whatever is easiest for you as long as you operate within the rules set out for your particular assessment.

You have to show competence throughout the assessment and you should therefore complete all of the tasks. Don't leave questions unanswered.

In some assessments written or complex tasks may be human marked. In this case you are given a blank space or table to enter your answer into. You are told in the assessments

which tasks these are (note: there may be none if all answers are marked by the computer).

If these involve calculations, it is a good idea to decide in advance how you are going to lay out your answers to such tasks by practising answering them on a word document, and certainly you should try all such tasks in this question bank and in the AAT's environment using the sample/practice assessments.

When asked to fill in tables, or gaps, never leave any blank even if you are unsure of the answer. Fill in your best estimate.

Note that for some assessments where there is a lot of scenario information or tables of data provided (eg tax tables), you may need to access these via 'pop-ups'. Instructions will be provided on how you can bring up the necessary data during the assessment.

Finally, take note of any task specific instructions once you are in the assessment. For example you may be asked to enter a date in a certain format or to enter a number to a certain number of decimal places.

Remember you can practise the BPP questions in this question bank in an online environment on our dedicated AAT Online page. On the same page is a link to the current AAT Sample Assessments as well.

If you have any comments about this book, please e-mail nisarahmed@bpp.com or write to Nisar Ahmed, AAT Head of Programme, BPP Learning Media Ltd, BPP House, Aldine Place, London W12 8AA.

Question bank

Costs and Revenues Question bank

Chapter 1 Introduction to cost accounting

Task 1.1

Drag and drop the correct answers into the table below:

1. Annual
2. When required
3. External to the organisation
4. Historic
5. Internal management
6. Specified by law
7. To be useful
8. Historic and future

	Financial accounting	Management accounting
Users		
Timing		
Type of information		
Format		

Task 1.2

Drag and drop the correct answers into the table below:

1. Prime cost
2. Materials
3. Production overheads
4. Production cost
5. Non-production overheads
6. Total cost

COST CARD		£
Direct [ ]		X
Direct labour		X
Direct expenses		X̲
[ ]		X
[ ]		X̲
[ ]		X
[ ]		
– selling and distribution		X
– administration		X
– finance		X̲
[ ]		X̲

Task 1.3

Which of the following would be classed as indirect labour?

☐ A coach driver in a transport company

☐ Machine operators in a milk bottling plant

☐ A maintenance assistant in a factory maintenance department

☐ Plumbers in a construction company

Task 1.4

For which of the following is a profit centre manager normally responsible?

☐ Cost only

☐ Costs and revenues

☐ Costs, revenues and investment

Task 1.5

Which of the following items would be treated as an indirect cost?

☐ Wood used to make a chair

☐ Metal used for the legs of a chair

☐ Fabric to cover the seat of a chair

☐ Staples to fix the fabric to the seat of a chair

Task 1.6

Prime cost is:

☐ All costs incurred in manufacturing a product

☐ The total of direct costs

☐ The material cost of a product

☐ The cost of operating a department

Task 1.7

You are an accounts assistant at J Co, a business which makes wooden toy soldiers. You have been asked to present a cost card for the toy soldiers using the following information.

Drag and drop the correct answers into the table below and insert the corresponding figures:

		£
1.	Rent, rates, light and heat	0.30
2.	Hire of special tools	0.50
3.	Toy makers' wages	3.00
4.	Advertising and sales promotion	0.70
5.	Wood and paint	3.50

COST CARD – TOY SOLDIER

£

Direct materials

Direct labour

Direct expenses

Prime cost

Production cost

Non-production overheads:

Total cost

Task 1.8

Which one of the following would be classed as a cost object?

☐ A branch of a high street retailer

☐ Labour in a staff canteen

☐ Rent paid on a factory

☐ Staples used in manufacturing a bed

Task 1.9

A company employs three drivers to deliver goods to its customers. The salaries paid to these drivers are:

☐ A part of prime cost

☐ A direct production expense

☐ A production overhead

☐ A selling and distribution overhead

Task 1.10

L Ltd is a badminton racquet manufacturer.

Drag and drop the correct entries into the box below to match the correct cost type to each cost item.

Selling and distribution costs

Direct materials

Indirect labour

Direct labour

Administration costs

Cost types	
Carbon for racquet heads	
Office stationery	
Wages of employees stringing racquets	
Supervisors' salaries	
Advertising stand at badminton tournaments	

Chapter 2 Cost classification and cost behaviour

Task 2.1

Drag and drop the correct entries into the table below, based on whether each one would be classified as a production cost, a selling and distribution cost or an administration cost:

- (a) Factory heat and light
- (b) Finance Director's salary
- (c) Sales Director's salary
- (d) Depreciation of delivery vans
- (e) Depreciation of plant and machinery
- (f) Fuel and oil for delivery vans

Cost types	
Production cost	
Selling and distribution cost	
Administration cost	

Task 2.2

Look at the two graphs below. **What costs do they depict?**

Graph A

☐ Variable cost per unit

☐ Fixed cost per unit

☐ Total fixed cost across level of activity

☐ Total variable cost

Graph B

☐ Variable cost per unit

☐ Fixed cost per unit

☐ Total fixed cost across level of activity

☐ Total variable cost

Graph A

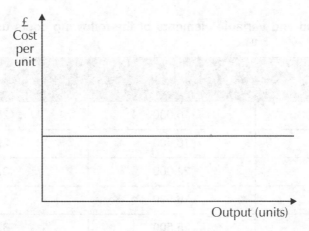

Graph B

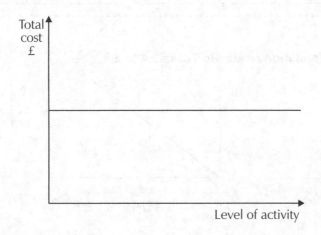

Task 2.3

Calculate the fixed and variable elements of the following costs using the high-low technique:

Month	Output (units)	Total cost (£)
January	16,000	252,500
February	18,500	290,000
March	24,000	372,500
April	26,500	410,000
May	25,500	395,000

The following information relates to Tasks 2.4 to 2.8

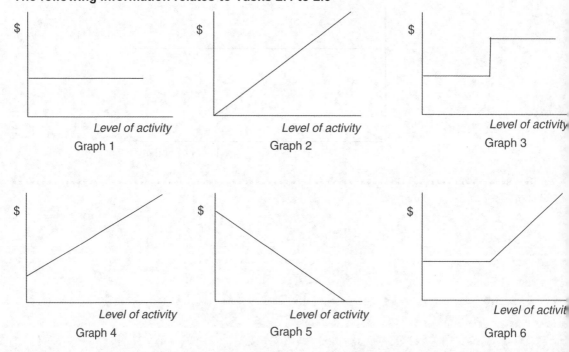

Graph 1

Graph 2

Graph 3

Graph 4

Graph 5

Graph 6

Which one of the above graphs illustrates the costs described in tasks 2.4 to 2.8?

Task 2.4

A variable cost – when the vertical axis represents cost incurred.

☐ Graph 1

☐ Graph 2

☐ Graph 4

☐ Graph 5

Task 2.5

A fixed cost – when the vertical axis represents cost incurred.

☐ Graph 1

☐ Graph 2

☐ Graph 3

☐ Graph 6

Task 2.6

A variable cost – when the vertical axis represents cost per unit.

☐ Graph 1

☐ Graph 2

☐ Graph 3

☐ Graph 6

Task 2.7

A semi-variable cost – when the vertical axis represents cost incurred.

☐ Graph 1

☐ Graph 2

☐ Graph 4

☐ Graph 5

Task 2.8

A step fixed cost – when the vertical axis represents cost incurred.

- [ ] Graph 3
- [ ] Graph 4
- [ ] Graph 5
- [ ] Graph 6

Task 2.9

A company has recorded the following data in the two most recent periods.

Total costs of production £	Volume of production Units
13,500	700
18,300	1,100

What is the best estimate of the company's fixed costs per period?

- [ ] £13,500
- [ ] £13,200
- [ ] £5,100
- [ ] £4,800

Task 2.10

We usually classify short-term costs into fixed, variable, step-fixed or semi-variable but in the long run, all costs are:

- [ ] Fixed
- [ ] Variable
- [ ] Step-fixed
- [ ] Semi-variable

Task 2.11

The following information is available for product Zed for the month of January.

Production costs:

Variable   £8 per unit

Fixed   £12,000

What is the total production cost of producing 8,000 units of product Zed in January?

£ _____ .

....

Chapter 3 Material costs and inventory valuation

Task 3.1

Paris Ltd manufactures a product the Lipsy, which requires plastic handles PH5:

- Annual demand 90,000 kilograms
- Annual holding cost per kilogram £1
- Fixed ordering cost £2

(a) **Calculate the Economic Order Quantity (EOQ) for PH5**

The inventory record shown below for plastic grade PH5 for the month of September has only been fully completed for the first three weeks of the month.

(b) **Complete the entries in the inventory record for the two receipts on 24 and 28 September that were ordered using the EOQ method.**

(c) **Complete ALL entries in the inventory record for the two issues in the month and for the closing balance at the end of September using the FIFO method of issuing inventory. (Show the costs per kilogram (kg) in £s to 3 decimal places; and the total costs in whole £s.)**

Inventory record for plastic grade PH5:

Date	Receipts			Issues			Balance	
	Quantity kg	Cost per kg (£)	Total cost (£)	Quantity kg	Cost per kg (£)	Total cost (£)	Quantity kg	Total cost (£)
Balance as at 22 September							150	180
24 September		1.398						
26 September				400				
28 September		1.402						
30 September				500				

Task 3.2

Calculate the closing inventory value at 31 March using FIFO by completing the entries in the inventory record below. Enter the cost per unit to 1 decimal place and the total cost to the nearest whole pound.

Inventory record

Date	Receipts			Issues			Balance	
	Quantity kg	Cost per kg (£)	Total cost (£)	Quantity kg	Cost per kg (£)	Total cost (£)	Quantity kg	Total cost (£)
Balance as at 1 January							4,000	10,000
31 January	1,000		2,000					
15 February				3,000		7,500		
28 February	1,500		3,750					
14 March				500		1,250		

Task 3.3

Using the AVCO method calculate the cost of materials issues and the value of closing inventory using the information below.

Enter your answer onto the inventory record below. Important! Enter the cost per kg to 2 decimal places. Enter the total cost to the nearest whole pound.

1 January	Balance	300 kg	£25 per unit
2 January	Issue	250 kg	
12 January	Receipt	400 kg	£25.75 per unit
21 January	Issue	200 kg	
29 January	Issue	75 kg	

	Inventory Record Card								
	Purchases			Requisitions			Balance		
Date	Quantity (kg)	Cost £	Total cost £	Quantity (kg)	Cost £	Total cost £	Quantity (kg)	Total cost £	
1 Jan									
2 Jan									
12 Jan									
21 Jan									
29 Jan									

Task 3.4

Fill in the table below using FIFO to calculate the closing valuation at 31 March.

Inventory record

Date	Receipts			Issues			Balance	
	Quantity kg	Cost per kg (£)	Total cost (£)	Quantity kg	Cost per kg (£)	Total cost (£)	Quantity kg	Total cost (£)
1 January	4,000	2.50	10,000				4,000	10,000
31 January	1,000		2,000					
15 February				3,000				
28 February	1,500	2.50					3,500	8,250
14 March				500				

Task 3.5

Fill in the table below using LIFO to calculate the closing valuation at 31 March.

Inventory record

Date	Receipts			Issues			Balance	
	Quantity kg	Cost per kg (£)	Total cost (£)	Quantity kg	Cost per kg (£)	Total cost (£)	Quantity kg	Total cost (£)
1 January	4,000	2.50	10,000				4,000	10,000
31 January	1,000	2.00						
15 February				3,000				
28 February	1,500	2.50						
14 March				500				

Task 3.6

A company wishes to minimise its inventory costs. Order costs are £10 per order and holding costs are £0.10 per unit per month. Fall Co estimates **annual** demand to be 5,400 units.

The economic order quantity is [ ] **units**.

Task 3.7

The following data relates to component L512:

Ordering costs	£100 per order
Inventory holding costs	£8 per unit per annum
Annual demand	1,225 units

The economic order quantity is [ ] **units (to the nearest whole unit).**

Task 3.8

The following data relate to inventory item A452:

Average usage	100 units per day
Minimum usage	60 units per day
Maximum usage	130 units per day
Lead time	20-26 days
EOQ	4,000 units

The maximum inventory level was [   ] **units**.

Chapter 4 Labour costs and expenses

Task 4.1

Below is a weekly timesheet for one of Paris Ltd's employees, who is paid as follows:

- For a basic seven-hour shift every day from Monday to Friday – basic pay.

- For any overtime in excess of the basic seven hours, on any day from Monday to Friday – the extra hours are paid at time-and-a-third (basic pay plus an overtime premium equal to a third of basic pay).

- For three contracted hours each Saturday morning – basic pay.

- For any hours in excess of three hours on Saturday – the extra hours are paid at double time (basic pay plus an overtime premium equal to basic pay).

- For any hours worked on Sunday – paid at double time (basic pay plus an overtime premium equal to basic pay).

Complete the columns headed Basic pay, Overtime premium and Total pay:

(Notes: Zero figures should be entered in cells where appropriate; Overtime pay is the premium amount paid for the extra hours worked).

Employee's weekly timesheet for week ending 14 May

	Hours spent on production	Hours worked on indirect work	Notes	Basic pay £	Overtime premium £	Total pay £
Monday	6	1	10am-11am setting up of machinery			
Tuesday	3	4	9am-1pm department meeting			
Wednesday	8					
Thursday	8					
Friday	6	1	3pm-4pm health and safety training			
Saturday	4					
Sunday	4					
Total	**39**	**6**				

Employee: H. Hector   **Cost Centre:** Lipsy calibration

Employee number: LP100   **Basic pay per hour:** £9.00

Task 4.2

Paris Ltd is reviewing its overtime payments for employees and has decided to increase basic pay from £9/hr to £10/hr and reduce its payment of overtime as follows. All other terms remain the same.

- For any overtime in excess of the basic seven hours, on any day from Monday to Friday – the extra hours are paid at time-and-a-quarter (basic pay plus an overtime premium equal to a quarter of basic pay).

- For four contracted hours each Saturday morning – basic pay.

- For any hours worked on Sunday – paid at time and a half (basic pay plus an overtime premium equal to half of basic pay).

Recalculate the timesheet for H. Hector for the week ending 14 May, taking these changes into account.

Employee: H. Hector			Cost Centre: Lipsy calibration			
Employee number: LP100			Basic pay per hour: £10.00			
	Hours spent on production	Hours worked on indirect work	Notes	Basic pay £	Overtime premium £	Total pay £
Monday	6	1	10am-11am setting up of machinery			
Tuesday	3	4	9am-1pm department meeting			
Wednesday	8					
Thursday	8					
Friday	6	1	3pm-4pm health and safety training			
Saturday	4					
Sunday	4					
Total	39	6				

Task 4.3

Paris Ltd has drawn up its payroll records for the month of May. The records show the following details of pay:

	£
Net pay	250,000
PAYE and NIC deductions	62,500
Contributions to company welfare scheme	37,500
Gross pay	350,000

The payroll analysis shows that £275,000 relates to direct labour, and £75,000 is for indirect labour. **The Financial controller has asked you to record the entries in the ledger in the Wages control account.** Remember Paris Ltd is a manufacturing company, so you need to think about work in progress too. Use the dropdown boxes to enter the line items and enter the relevant figures.

Wages control account

	£		£
Picklist 1	▼	Picklist 4	▼
Picklist 2	▼	Picklist 5	
Picklist 3	▼		

Picklist 1

Bank
WIP
Production overhead control

Picklist 2

HM Revenue and Customs
WIP

Picklist 3

Welfare scheme contributions
Production overhead control

Picklist 4

Bank
WIP
HM Revenue and Customs

Picklist 5

Bank
Welfare scheme contributions
Production overhead control
HM Revenue and Customs

Task 4.4

The ledger clerk has forgotten to complete the other entries needed for wages in the work in progress control account and the production overhead control account. **Input the correct entries in the two control accounts below.** Remember that £275,000 relates to direct labour and £75,000 to indirect labour.

Work in progress control account

		£			£
31 May	Wages control				

Production overhead control

		£			£
31 May	Wages control				

Task 4.5

Which one of the following groups of workers would be classified as indirect labour?

☐ Machinists in an organisation manufacturing clothes

☐ Bricklayers in a house building company

☐ Maintenance workers in a shoe factory

Task 4.6

In a typical cost ledger, the double entry for indirect labour cost incurred is:

☐	DEBIT	Wages control	CREDIT	Overhead control
☐	DEBIT	Admin overhead control	CREDIT	Wages control
☐	DEBIT	Overhead control	CREDIT	Wages control
☐	DEBIT	Wages control	CREDIT	Admin overhead control

Task 4.7

Extracts are given below from Gloworm Ltd's payroll for March.

Manufacturing department A production employees' wages	£18,500
Manufacturing department B production employees' wages	£22,500
Maintenance department employees' wages	£12,700
General admin department employees' salaries	£7,600

Complete the cost journal entries to record the payroll payments for March.

	Code	Dr £	Cr £
Manufacturing department A wages	▼		
Manufacturing department A wages	▼		
Manufacturing department B wages	▼		
Manufacturing department B wages	▼		
Maintenance department wages	▼		
Maintenance department wages	▼		
General admin department salaries	▼		
General admin department salaries	▼		

Picklist:

2300 Manufacturing department A direct costs
2400 Manufacturing department B direct costs
3400 Operating overheads
3500 Non-operating overheads
6000 Wages control account

··

Task 4.8

In a typical cost ledger, the double entry for direct wages cost incurred is:

☐	DEBIT	Wages control	CREDIT	Work-in-progress account
☐	DEBIT	Work-in-progress account	CREDIT	Wages control
☐	DEBIT	Costs of sales account	CREDIT	Work-in-progress account
☐	DEBIT	Finished goods account	CREDIT	Work-in-progress account

··

Task 4.9

Below is a table showing the hours worked by one of XYZ Ltd's employees, who is paid as follows:

- For a basic shift every day from Monday to Friday, the basic pay is £15 per hour.

- For any overtime in excess of the basic hours, on any day from Monday to Friday – the extra hours are paid at time-and-a-half (basic pay plus an overtime premium equal to half of basic pay).

- For any hours worked on Saturday or Sunday the hours are paid at double time (basic pay plus an overtime premium equal to basic pay).

(a) **Complete the gaps in the table below to calculate the labour cost (to 2 decimal places)**.

Employee's weekly timesheet for week ending 7 December

	Hours	Total pay £
Basic pay (including basic hours for overtime)	48	
Mon-Fri overtime premium	7	
Sat-Sun overtime premium	6	
Total		

(b) Employees are also entitled to a bonus of 30% of basic hourly rate for every unit pf production in excess of the monthly target. The target for last month was 450 units and employee A produced 480 units.

What was employee A's bonus payment for the month? £ ⬚

(c) At the end of the month there was a total closing work-in-progress of 7,000 units which were 60% complete with regard to labour.

What are the equivalent units of production with regard to labour of the closing work-in-progress? ⬚ **units**.

Task 4.10

ABC Ltd produced 42,000 equivalent units of production in June. The total direct labour cost for June was £13,650.

Calculate the total direct labour cost per equivalent unit of the finished production for June.

Give your answer in £s to three decimal places.

£ ☐

....

Chapter 5 Accounting for overheads

Task 5.1

Paris Ltd has set its budgets and estimated its budgeted overheads and activity levels as follows:

	Silicon moulding	Silicon extrusion
Budgeted overheads (£)	450,000	352,520
Budgeted direct labour hours	25,350	20,475
Budgeted machine hours	8,750	6,350

(a) **What would be the budgeted overhead absorption rate for each department, if this were set based on their both being heavily automated?**

☐ Silicon moulding £18/hour, Silicon extrusion £17/hour
☐ Silicon moulding £51/hour, Silicon extrusion £17/hour
☐ Silicon moulding £51/hour, Silicon extrusion £56/hour
☐ Silicon moulding £18/hour, Silicon extrusion £56/hour

(b) **What would be the budgeted overhead absorption rate for each department, if this were set based on their both being labour intensive?**

☐ Silicon moulding £51/hour, Silicon extrusion £17/hour
☐ Silicon moulding £18/hour, Silicon extrusion £17/hour
☐ Silicon moulding £18/hour, Silicon extrusion £56/hour
☐ Silicon moulding £51/hour, Silicon extrusion £56/hour

Additional data

At the end of the quarter actual overheads incurred were found to be:

	Silicon moulding	Silicon extrusion
Actual overheads (£)	425,799	354,416

(c) **Assuming that exactly the same amount of overheads was absorbed as budgeted, what were the under- or over-absorptions in the quarter?**

☐ Silicon moulding over-absorbed £24,201, Silicon extrusion over-absorbed £1,896

☐ Silicon moulding over-absorbed £24,201, Silicon extrusion under-absorbed £1,896

☐ Silicon moulding under-absorbed £24,201, Silicon extrusion under-absorbed £1,896

☐ Silicon moulding under-absorbed £24,201, Silicon extrusion over-absorbed £1,896

Task 5.2

The financial controller at Paris Ltd has looked at the overhead absorption rates in the two cost centres, and wants a single rate for labour hours and for machinery across the two centres. She has chosen £20/hr for labour hours and £55/hr for machinery.

Recalculate the budgeted direct labour hours and machine hours based on these rates. Give your answers to the nearest whole number. Refer to the table below from the last task:

	Silicon moulding	Silicon extrusion
Budgeted overheads (£)	450,000	352,520
Budgeted direct labour hours		
Budgeted machine hours		

Task 5.3

(a) **At the end of the quarter you have been asked to recalculate the overhead absorbed using the new rates and the following actual hours for labour and machinery:**

	Silicon moulding	Silicon extrusion
Actual direct labour hours	21,222	17,144
Actual machine hours	8,459	6,501
Overhead absorbed – labour hrs		
Overhead absorbed – machine hrs		

(b) **Using the actual overheads in Task 5.1, calculate any differences between the actual overheads at the end of the quarter and the overheads absorbed that you have just calculated.**

	Silicon moulding	Silicon extrusion
Actual overheads (£)		
Difference – labour hours		
Difference – machine hours		

Task 5.4

Over-absorbed overheads always occur when:

☐ Absorbed overheads exceed actual overheads

☐ Absorbed overheads exceed budgeted overheads

☐ Actual overheads exceed budgeted overheads

The following information relates to Tasks 5.5 and 5.6

A company has the following actual and budgeted data for year 4.

	Budget	Actual
Labour hours	8,000 hrs	9,000 hrs
Variable production overhead per unit	£3	£3
Fixed production overheads	£360,000	£432,000
Sales	6,000 units	8,000 units

Overheads are absorbed using a rate per unit, based on budgeted labour hours.

Task 5.5

The fixed production overhead absorbed during year 4 was:

☐ £384,000

☐ £405,000

☐ £432,000

☐ £459,000

Task 5.6

Fixed production overhead was:

☐ Under absorbed by £27,000

☐ Under absorbed by £72,000

☐ Under absorbed by £75,000

☐ Over absorbed by £27,000

Chapter 6 Absorption costing

Task 6.1

Paris Ltd's budgeted overheads for the next financial year are:

	£	£
Depreciation of plant and equipment		2,010,375
Power for production machinery		1,787,500
Rent and rates		261,268
Light and heat		57,750
Indirect labour costs:		
Maintenance	253,750	
Stores	90,125	
General Administration	600,251	
Total indirect labour cost		944,126

The following information is also available:

Department	Net book value of plant and equipment	Production machinery power usage (KwH)	Floor space (square metres)	Number of employees
Production centres:				
Silicon moulding	3,600,000	1,145,000		15
Silicon extrusion	4,400,000	2,430,000		16
Support cost centres:				
Maintenance			8,000	4
Stores			10,000	5
General Administration			10,000	6
Total	8,000,000	3,575,000	28,000	46

Overheads are allocated or apportioned on the most appropriate basis. The total overheads of the support cost centres are then reapportioned to the two production centres using the direct method.

- 35% of the Maintenance cost centre's time is spent maintaining production machinery in the Silicon moulding production centre, and the remainder in the Silicon extrusion production centre.

- The Stores cost centre makes 40% of its issues to the Silicon moulding production centre, and 60% to the Silicon extrusion production centre.

- General Administration supports the two production centres equally.

- There is no reciprocal servicing between the three support cost centres.

Complete the table showing the apportionment and reapportionment of overheads to the two production centres. Round to the nearest pound.

	Basis of apportionment	Silicon moulding £	Silicon extrusion £	Maintenance £	Stores £	General Admin £	Totals £
Depreciation of plant and equipment	NBV of Plant and equipment						
Power for production machinery	Production machinery power usage (KwH)						
Rent and rates	Floor space						
Light and heat	Floor space						
Indirect labour	Allocated						
Totals							
Reapportion Maintenance							
Reapportion Stores							
Reapportion General Admin							
Total overheads to production centres							

Task 6.2

(a) The financial controller at Paris Ltd is reviewing the basis of allocating the costs of the two production centres, and is considering using the number of employees instead of NBV and power usage. **Recalculate the allocations and apportionments using headcount as a basis for these two cost centres. She has also decided that the silicon moulding cost centre uses far more general admin than the extrusion cost centre, and wants you to recalculate the apportionments using a ratio of 65:35.** Use the dropdown screen to remind you of the data in the task.

Dropdown screen

Paris Ltd's budgeted overheads for the next financial year are:

	£	£
Depreciation of plant and equipment		2,010,375
Power for production machinery		1,787,500
Rent and rates		261,268
Light and heat		57,750
Indirect labour costs:		
Maintenance	253,750	
Stores	90,125	
General Administration	600,251	
Total indirect labour cost		944,126

The following information is also available:

Department	Net book value of plant and equipment	Production machinery power usage (KwH)	Floor space (square metres)	Number of employees
Production centres:				
Silicon moulding	3,600,000	1,145,000		15
Silicon extrusion	4,400,000	2,430,000		16
Support cost centres:				
Maintenance			8,000	4
Stores			10,000	5
General Administration			10,000	6
Total	8,000,000	3,575,000	28,000	46

Overheads are allocated or apportioned on the most appropriate basis. The total overheads of the support cost centres are then reapportioned to the two production centres using the direct method.

- 35% of the Maintenance cost centre's time is spent maintaining production machinery in the Silicon moulding production centre, and the remainder in the Silicon extrusion production centre.

- The Stores cost centre makes 40% of its issues to the Silicon moulding production centre, and 60% to the Silicon extrusion production centre.

- General Administration supports the two production centres, with 65% of its costs attributable to Silicon moulding and 35% attributable to Silicon extrusion.

- There is no reciprocal servicing between the three support cost centres.

Complete the table showing the apportionment and reapportionment of overheads to the two production centres.

	Basis of apportionment	Silicon moulding £	Silicon extrusion £	Mainten ance £	Stores £	General Admin £	Totals £
Depreciation of plant and equipment	Headcount						
Power for production machinery	Headcount						
Rent and rates	Floor space						
Light and heat	Floor space						
Indirect labour	Allocated						
Totals							
Reapportion Maintenance							
Reapportion Stores							
Reapportion General Admin							
Total overheads to production centres							

(b) **If you were the manager in charge of the silicon moulding cost centre would you be happy with the revised allocations?**

Task 6.3

Product Em has the following estimated costs per unit.

Product Em	£ per unit
Direct materials	5.50
Direct labour	7.20
Variable overheads	1.50
Fixed manufacturing overheads	2.30
Fixed administration, selling and distribution costs	1.70
Total costs	18.20

What is the full absorption cost of one unit of Em?

£ _____

....

Chapter 7 Job, batch and service costing

Task 7.1

Drag and drop the correct entries into the box below to match the correct cost unit to a service:

1. Occupied bed-night
2. Patient-day
3. Meal served
4. Passenger/kilometre, tonne/kilometre
5. Full-time student

Service	Cost unit
Road, rail and air transport services	
Hotels	
Education	
Hospitals	
Catering establishments	

Task 7.2

Petra Jones is a builder who has issued a quote for a conservatory. Now the job is completed, she would like you to calculate any variances that have arisen. **State whether each variance is favourable or adverse (unfavourable).** The details are in the table below. Input your answers into the right hand column.

Job number 03456

	Budget £	Actual £	Variance F/A £
Direct materials			
Plasterboard	3,600.00	3,500.00	
Wood & door frames	4,750.00	4,802.00	
Insulation	1,050.00	1,145.00	
Electrical fittings	320.00	300.00	
Windows	2,220.00	2,576.00	
Paint	270.00	250.00	
Direct labour			
Construction	554.00	641.00	
Electrical	224.00	160.00	

	Budget £	Actual £	Variance F/A £
Decorating	165.00	205.00	
Direct expenses			
Hire of specialist lathe	240.00	240.00	
Overheads (based on direct lab hrs)			
84/90 hours @ £15.00	1,260.00	1,350.00	

Task 7.3

(a) **Petra Jones has also asked you to highlight any variances above 5% for further investigation. Use the table below to make your calculations. Enter the percentages to one decimal place.**

(b) **She also wants you to calculate the profit on the job, comparing this with the original quotation made based on 20% of total cost.**

(c) **Calculate the percentage variance between the original profit and the final profit figure. Give your answer to 1 decimal place.**

☐ %

	Budget £	Actual £	Variance F/A £	%
Direct materials				
Plasterboard	3,600.00	3,500.00	100F	
Wood & door frames	4,750.00	4,802.00	52A	
Insulation	1,050.00	1,145.00	95A	
Electrical fittings	320.00	300.00	20F	
Windows	2,220.00	2,576.00	356A	
Paint	270.00	250.00	20F	
Direct labour				
Construction	554.00	641.00	87A	
Electrical	224.00	160.00	64F	
Decorating	165.00	205.00	40A	
Direct expenses				
Hire of specialist lathe	240.00	240.00	0	
Overheads (based on direct lab hrs)				
84/90 hours @ £15.00	1,260.00	1,350.00	90A	
Total cost	14,653.00			
Profit	2,930.60			
Net price	17,583.60			
VAT at 20%	3,516.72			
Total price	21,100.32			

Task 7.4

Which of the following are characteristics of service costing?

- [ ] High levels of indirect costs as a proportion of total cost
- [ ] Cost units are often intangible
- [ ] Use of composite cost units
- [ ] Use of equivalent units

Task 7.5

Product Tee is made in batches of 32,000 units and the following costs are estimated.

Product Tee	£ per batch
Direct materials	176,000
Direct labour	230,400
Variable overheads	48,000
Fixed manufacturing overheads	73,600
Fixed administration, selling and distribution costs	54,400
Total costs	582,400

(a) **Calculate the total cost of one unit of product Tee.**

£ ☐

(b) **Calculate the full absorption cost of one unit of product Tee.**

£ ☐

(c) **Calculate the full absorption cost of one batch of product Tee.**

£ ☐

Chapter 8 Process costing

Task 8.1

The teeming and lading department of Paris Ltd uses process costing for some of its products.

The process account for October for one particular process has been partly completed but the following information is also relevant:

Two employees worked on this process during October. Each employee worked 37 hours per week for 4 weeks and was paid £12.50 per hour.

Overheads are absorbed on the basis of £10.50 per labour hour.

Paris Ltd expects a normal loss of 10% during this process, which it then sells for scrap at 60p per kg.

(a) **Complete the process account below for December.**

Description	Kg	Unit cost £	Total cost £	Description	Kg	Unit cost £	Total cost £
Material TL4	700	1.35		Normal loss		0.60	
Material TL3	350	1.50		Output			
Material TL9	400	1.25					
Labour							
Overheads							

(b) **Identify the correct journal entries for an abnormal loss.**

	Debit	Credit
Abnormal loss account		
Process account		

Task 8.2

Paris Ltd has reviewed its labour costs and decided to hire two cheaper employees, paying them £9.50 per hour. However they are less experienced and take longer, so they each work 40 hours per week for four weeks. The normal loss goes up to 20% during the process. Overheads continue to be absorbed at £10.50 per labour hour.

Recalculate the process account to take account of these changes.

Description	Kg	Unit cost £	Total cost £	Description	Kg	Unit cost £	Total cost £
Material TL4	700	1.35		Normal loss		0.60	
Material TL3	350	1.50		Output			
Material TL9	400	1.25					
Labour							
Overheads							

Do you think the decision made by management is a good one?

Task 8.3

Paris Ltd makes a product which goes through several processes. The following information is available for the month of June:

	Kg
Opening WIP	4,500
Input	54,300
Normal loss	400
Transferred to finished goods	60,400

What was the abnormal gain in June?

☐ 2,600 kg

☐ 3,000 kg

☐ 2,000 kg

☐ 2,560 kg

Task 8.4

A food manufacturing process has a normal wastage of 10% of input. In a period, 3,000 kg of material were input and there was an abnormal loss of 75 kg. No inventories are held at the beginning or end of the process.

The quantity of good production achieved was ⬚ **kg.**

Task 8.5

A company makes a product, which passes through a single process.

Details of the process for the last period are as follows:

Materials   5,000 kg at 50p per kg

Normal losses are 10% of input in the process, and without further processing any losses can be sold as scrap for 20p per kg.

The output for the period was 4,200 kg from the process.

There was no work in progress at the beginning or end of the period.

(a) **The value credited to the process account for the scrap value of the normal loss for the period will be £** ⬚ (to the nearest £).

(b) **The abnormal loss for the period is** ⬚ **kg.**

Task 8.6

What is an equivalent unit?

(a) A unit of output which is identical to all others manufactured in the same process

(b) Notional whole units used to represent uncompleted work

(c) A unit of product in relation to which costs are ascertained

(d) The amount of work achievable, at standard efficiency levels, in an hour

---

Task 8.7

G Ltd has a process called H4. During the month of June the costs of that process were £56,000 and the output was 20,400 completed units and 8,000 units that were 25% completed.

What is the cost per equivalent unit?

Task 8.8

(a) Another of G Ltd's processes is the C4. The costs incurred in this process for the month of June are as follows:

Materials	£21,600
Labour and overheads	£13,350

At the end of the period there were 8,300 units of completed output and 1,000 units of closing work in progress. The work in progress has had 70% of its material input and 60% of the labour and overheads input.

Calculate the cost per equivalent unit for materials and labour/overheads.

	Units	Materials Proportion complete	Equivalent units	Labour/overheads Proportion complete	Equivalent units
Completed		100%		100%	
Work in progress		70%		60%	
Total equivalent units					
Cost per equivalent unit	=		-	=	-

(b) Find values for the completed output and the closing work in progress.

£

Completed output	
Materials	
Labour/overhead	
Work in progress	
Materials	
Labour/overhead	

Task 8.9

Beeb Ltd has the following costs in a period:

Raw materials 4,100 units	£45,100
Labour	£32,608
Overheads	£16,424

Opening WIP: 100 units with a value of £1,220. It was 100% complete for materials, 60% for labour and 30% for overheads.

The split of the £1,220 is:

Materials	£800
Labour	£360
Overheads	£60
	£1,220

Output from this Process: 4,040 units

Closing WIP: 160 units with a value of £2,912. It was also complete as below:

Raw materials	100%	complete
Labour	60%	complete
Overheads	60%	complete

There were no losses.

Required

Prepare a statement of equivalent units using FIFO.

(a) **FIFO**

Statement of equivalent units

	Actual Units	Materials	Equivalent Units Labour	Overheads
Opening WIP				
Goods started and finished				
Good output				
Closing WIP				
Equivalent units				

(b) **Prepare a statement of cost per equivalent unit**

	£	£	£
Input costs			
Cost per equivalent unit			

(c) **Value the units**

Value of good output =   Costs b/f in opening WIP =

Materials

Labour

Overheads

£

Value of Closing WIP =

(d) **Prepare the process account**

Process

	Units	£		Units	£
Opening WIP b/f			Good output		
Raw Materials					
Labour			Closing WIP		
Overheads					

Task 8.10

Beeb Ltd has the following costs in a period:

Raw materials 4,100 units	£45,100
Labour	£32,608
Overheads	£16,424

Opening WIP: 100 units with a value of £1,220. It was 100% complete for materials, 60% for labour and 30% for overheads.

The split of the £1,220 is:

Materials	£800
Labour	£360
Overheads	£60
	£1,220

Output from this Process: 4,040 units

Closing WIP: 160 units with a value of £2,912. It was also complete as below:

Raw materials	100%	complete
Labour	60%	complete
Overheads	60%	complete

There were no losses.

Required

(a) Prepare a statement of equivalent units using the weighted average method.

Statement of equivalent units

	Actual units	Materials	Equivalent units Labour	Overheads
Good output				
Closing WIP				
Equivalent units				

(b) **Prepare a statement of cost per equivalent unit**

	£	£	£
Costs b/f			
Input costs			
Cost per equivalent unit =			
Input costs/Equivalent units			
(to 2dp)			

Total =

(c) **Value the units**

Value of good output (to 0 dp) =

Value of Closing WIP (to 0 dp) =

(d) **Prepare the process account**

Process

	Units	£		Units	£
Opening WIP b/f			Output W1		
Raw Materials			Closing WIP c/d		
Labour					
Overheads			Rounding		(21)

Chapter 9 Budgeting: fixed and flexed budgets

Task 9.1

Paris Ltd has prepared a forecast for the next quarter for one of its small components, PA01. This component is produced in batches, and the forecast is based on producing and selling 3,000 batches.

One of the customers of Paris Ltd has indicated that it may be significantly increasing its order level for component PA01 for the next quarter, and it appears that activity levels of 3,750 batches and 5,000 batches are feasible.

The semi-variable costs should be calculated using the high-low method. If 7,500 batches are sold the total semi-variable cost will be £18,450, and there is a constant unit variable cost up to this volume.

Complete the table below and calculate the estimated profit per batch of PA01 at the different activity levels.

Batches produced and sold	3,000	3,750	5,000
	£	£	£
Sales revenue	60,000		
Variable costs:			
• Direct materials	5,700		
• Direct labour	27,000		
• Overheads	9,300		
Semi-variable costs:	9,450		
• Variable element			
• Fixed element			
Total cost	51,450		
Total profit	8,550		
Profit per batch (to 2 decimal places)	2.85		

Task 9.2

(a) The financial controller at Paris Ltd has just informed you of the following cost increases and asked you to recalculate the budget at the three activity levels.

Direct materials £2.00/kg. 1 kg is used in each PA01.

Direct labour £10/hr. It takes 1 hour to make a PA01.

Overheads are now £3.20 per PA01.

Complete the table below and calculate the estimated profit per batch of PA01 at the different activity levels.

Batches produced and sold	3,000	3,750	5,000
	£	£	£
Sales revenue	60,000		
Variable costs:			
• Direct materials			
• Direct labour			
• Overheads			
Semi-variable costs:	9,450		
• Variable element			
• Fixed element			
Total cost			
Total profit			
Profit per batch (to 2 decimal places)			

BPP
LEARNING MEDIA

Task 9.3

A customer has put in an order for 4,000 batches. Production is stopped where the profit per batch is less than £2. Recommend to management whether Paris Ltd should go ahead with the order. **Fill in the table below:**

Batches produced and sold	3,000	4,000
	£	£
Sales revenue	60,000	
Variable costs:		
• Direct materials	6,000	
• Direct labour	30,000	
• Overheads	9,600	
Semi-variable costs:		
• Variable element	6,000	
• Fixed element	3,450	
Total cost	55,050	
Total profit	4,950	
Profit per batch (to 2 decimal places)	1.65	

Choose the correct option below.

Paris Ltd should accept/reject the order for 4,000 units.

··

Chapter 10 Variance analysis

Task 10.1

Paris Ltd has the following original budget and actual performance for product SHEP for the year ending 30 September:

	Budget	Actual
Volume sold	150,000	156,000
	£'000	£'000
Sales revenue	1,200	1,326
Less costs:		
Direct materials	375	372
Direct labour	450	444
Overheads	225	250
Operating profit	150	260

Both direct materials and direct labour are variable costs, but the overheads are fixed.

Complete the table below to show a flexed budget and the resulting variances against this budget for the year. Show the actual variance amount for sales, each cost, and operating profit, in the column headed 'Variance' and indicate whether this is Favourable or Adverse by entering F or A in the final column. If neither F nor A enter 0.

	Flexed Budget	Actual	Variance	Favourable F or Adverse A
Volume sold		156,000		
	£'000	£'000	£'000	
Sales revenue		1,326		
Less costs:				
Direct materials		372		
Direct labour		444		
Overheads		250		
Operating profit		260		

Task 10.2

The Managing director of Paris Ltd has asked you to explain why the actual outcome was better than budgeted. He wants you to do some calculations and suggest reasons why the revenues and costs may be better than budgeted.

Input your calculations to two decimal places into the table below, in the two right hand columns. Ignore overheads.

	Flexed Budget	Actual	Budget unit cost/revenue	Actual unit cost/revenue
Volume sold	156,000	156,000		
	£'000	£'000		
Sales revenue	1,248	1,326		
Less costs:				
Direct materials	390	372		
Direct labour	468	444		
Overheads	225	250		
Operating profit	165	260		

Are the following true or false?

The unit selling price difference may be due to a rise in the sales price not planned in the budget.

True/False

The unit selling price difference may be due to fewer bulk discounts to customers.

True/False

The materials unit price difference may be due to bulk buying discounts.

True/False

The materials unit price difference may be due to a cheaper source of supply.

True/False

The labour cost difference may be due to having more lower paid employees.

True/False

The labour cost difference may be due to efficiency savings.

True/False

Chapter 11 Cost bookkeeping

Task 11.1

Drag and drop the correct entries into the journal below to record the following transactions:

1. Production overheads absorbed into production
2. Indirect labour transferred to production overheads
3. Completed WIP transferred to finished goods
4. Direct materials issued to production

The choices are:

Debit: WIP, Credit: Production overheads

Debit: Production overheads, Credit: Wages

Debit: Finished goods, Credit: WIP

Debit: WIP, Credit: Materials

Debit: WIP, Credit: Finished goods

Debit: Production overheads, Credit: WIP

Production overheads absorbed into production		
Indirect labour transferred to production overheads		
Completed WIP transferred to finished goods		
Direct materials issued to production		

BPP
LEARNING MEDIA

Task 11.2

Drag and drop the correct entries into the journal below to record the following transactions for overheads:

Transaction 1.   Over-absorbed: absorbed greater than incurred
Transaction 2.   Under-absorbed: incurred greater than absorbed

The drag and drop choices are:

- Debit: production overheads, Credit: statement of profit or loss
- Debit: statement of profit or loss, Credit: production overheads

	Drag and drop choice
Transaction 1	
Transaction 2	

....

Task 11.3

A company operates an integrated accounting system.

The accounting entries for the issue to production of indirect materials from inventory would be:

	DEBIT	*CREDIT*
☐	Work in progress account	Materials control account
☐	Materials control account	Production overhead control account
☐	Production overhead control account	Materials control account
☐	Cost of sales account	Materials control account

....

Chapter 12 Marginal costing

Task 12.1

Paris Ltd uses absorption costing, but is looking at adopting marginal costing across some of its products. The details for the PA121 are below:

Direct materials	£8.50
Direct labour	£17.00
Variable overheads	£3.00
Fixed overheads	£850,000

Overheads are absorbed on the machine hour basis, and it is estimated that in the next accounting period machine hours will total 250,000. Each unit requires two hours of machine time.

What is the cost per unit using:

(a) Absorption costing
(b) Marginal costing?

....

Task 12.2

Drag and drop the correct answer into the sentence below:

1. More for absorption costing
2. The same for both types of costing
3. Less for absorption costing

In the long run, total profit for a company will be [   ] whether marginal costing or absorption costing is used.

....

Task 12.3

Drag and drop the correct answer into the sentence below:

1. Absorption costing, marginal costing
2. Marginal costing, absorption costing

It might be argued that [   ] is preferable to [   ] **in management accounting**, in order to be consistent with the requirement of current accounting standards and financial reporting.

....

Task 12.4

Cost and selling price details for product Z are as follows.

	£
Direct materials	6.00
Direct labour	7.50
Variable overhead	2.50
Fixed overhead absorption rate	5.00
	21.00
Profit	9.00
Selling price	30.00

Budgeted production for the month was 5,000 units although the company managed to produce 5,800 units, selling 5,200 of them and incurring fixed overhead costs of £27,400.

(a) **What was the marginal costing profit for the month?**

☐ £45,400 ☐ £53,800

☐ £46,800 ☐ £72,800

(b) **What was the absorption costing profit for the month?**

☐ £45,200 ☐ £46,800

☐ £45,400 ☐ £48,400

Task 12.5

Product Dee is made in batches of 16,000 units and the following costs are estimated.

Product Dee	£ per batch
Direct materials	176,000
Direct labour	230,400
Variable overheads	48,000
Fixed manufacturing overheads	73,600
Fixed administration, selling and distribution costs	54,400
Total costs	582,400

(a) **Calculate the total cost of one unit of product Dee.**

£ ⬚

(b) **Calculate the full absorption cost of one unit of product Dee.**

£ ⬚

(c) **Calculate the full absorption cost of one batch of product Dee.**

£ ▢

(d) **Calculate the marginal cost of one batch of product Dee.**

£ ▢

(e) **Calculate the marginal cost of one unit of product Dee.**

£ ▢

Chapter 13 Short-term decision-making

Task 13.1

The COLIN has a selling price of £22 per unit with a total variable cost of £17 per unit. Paris Ltd estimates that the fixed costs per quarter associated with this product are £45,000.

(a) **Calculate the budgeted breakeven, in units, for product COLIN.**

units

(b) **Calculate the budgeted breakeven sales, in £s, for product COLIN.**

£

(c) **Complete the table below to show the budgeted margin of safety in units and the margin of safety percentage (to the nearest whole %) and the margin of safety in revenue if Paris Ltd sells 9,500 units or 10,500 units of product COLIN.**

Units of COLIN sold	9,500	10,500
Margin of safety (units)		
Margin of safety percentage		
Margin of safety revenue		

(d) **If Paris Ltd wishes to make a profit of £20,000, how many units of COLIN must it sell?**

units

(e) **If Paris Ltd increases the selling price of COLIN by £1 what will be the impact on the breakeven point and the margin of safety, assuming no change in the number of units sold?**

☐ The breakeven point will decrease and the margin of safety will increase.

☐ The margin of safety will stay the same but the breakeven point will increase.

☐ The breakeven point will decrease and the margin of safety will stay the same.

☐ The margin of safety will decrease and the breakeven point will decrease.

Task 13.2

(a) **Paris Ltd has decided to limit the production of the COLIN to 8,000 units per quarter. If the selling price and variable costs remain the same, what is the maximum fixed costs per quarter to breakeven? Remember the selling price is £22 per unit and the variable cost is £17 per unit.**

(b) **Calculate the revised budgeted breakeven, in £s, for product COLIN if fixed costs are £30,000 per quarter.**

£

(c) **Complete the table below to show the budgeted margin of safety in units and the margin of safety percentage (to the nearest whole %) if Paris Ltd sells 6,500 units or 7,000 units of product COLIN. Base this on your answer in part (b).**

Units of COLIN sold	6,500	7,000
	£	£
Margin of safety (units)		
Margin of safety percentage		

(d) **If Paris Ltd wishes to make a profit of £10,000, how many units of COLIN must it sell? Is it possible to make this level of profit? Base this on the data in parts (b) and (c).**

units

Task 13.3

A company makes a single product and incurs fixed costs of £30,000 per month. Variable cost per unit is £5 and each unit sells for £15. Monthly sales demand is 7,000 units.

The breakeven point in terms of monthly sales units is:

☐ 2,000 units

☐ 3,000 units

☐ 4,000 units

☐ 6,000 units

BPP
LEARNING MEDIA

Task 13.4

A company manufactures a single product for which cost and selling price data are as follows.

Selling price per unit   £12

Variable cost per unit   £8

Fixed costs per month   £96,000

Budgeted monthly sales   30,000 units

The margin of safety, expressed as a percentage of budgeted monthly sales, is (to the nearest whole number):

☐   20%

☐   25%

☐   73%

☐   125%

··

Task 13.5

Information concerning K Co's single product is as follows.

	£ per unit
Selling price	6.00
Variable production cost	1.20
Variable selling cost	0.40
Fixed production cost	4.00
Fixed selling cost	0.80

Budgeted production and sales for the year are 10,000 units.

(a)   **What is the company's breakeven point, to the nearest whole unit?**

☐   8,000 units

☐   8,333 units

☐   10,000 units

☐   10,909 units

(b) **How many units must be sold if K Co wants to achieve a profit of £11,000 for the year?**

☐ 2,500 units

☐ 9,833 units

☐ 10,625 units

☐ 13,409 units

Chapter 14 Long-term decision-making

Task 14.1

Beanie Ltd has a stamping machine nearing the end of its useful life and is considering purchasing a replacement machine.

Estimates have been made for the initial capital cost, sales income and operating costs of the replacement machine, which is expected to have a useful life of four years:

	Year 0 £'000	Year 1 £'000	Year 2 £'000	Year 3 £'000	Year 4 £'000
Capital expenditure	1,000				
Other cash flows:					
Sales income		350	400	400	350
Operating costs		100	110	120	130

The company appraises capital investment projects using a 11% cost of capital.

(a) **Complete the table below and calculate the net present value of the proposed replacement machine (to the nearest £'000):**

	Year 0 £'000	Year 1 £'000	Year 2 £'000	Year 3 £'000	Year 4 £'000
Capital expenditure					
Sales income					
Operating costs					
Net cash flows					
PV factors	1.0000	0.9009	0.8116	0.7312	0.6587
Discounted cash flows (to nearest £)					
Net present value					

The net present value is [▼]

Picklist:

Positive
Negative

(b) **Calculate the payback period of the proposed replacement machine to the nearest whole month.**

The payback period is [   ] year(s) and [   ] month(s).

··

Task 14.2

The Managing Director of Beanie Ltd has been looking at your calculations for the replacement machine. **He wants to know the maximum he should pay for a replacement machine to make sure the NPV at least breaks even.**

··

Task 14.3

It has now been decided to purchase the replacement stamping machine, but the managing director wants you to use a lower rate for the cost of capital and he has settled on 7%. He also wants you to use a figure of £810,000 for the cost of the replacement machine. All other cash flows are as before.

	Year 0 £'000	Year 1 £'000	Year 2 £'000	Year 3 £'000	Year 4 £'000
Capital expenditure	810				
Other cash flows:					
Sales income		350	400	400	350
Operating costs		100	110	120	130

The company appraises capital investment projects using a 7% cost of capital.

Complete the table below and calculate the net present value of the proposed replacement machine (to the nearest £'000):

	Year 0 £'000	Year 1 £'000	Year 2 £'000	Year 3 £'000	Year 4 £'000
Capital expenditure					
Sales income					
Operating costs					
Net cash flows					
PV factors	1.0000	0.9346	0.8734	0.8163	0.7629
Discounted cash flows (to nearest £)					
Net present value					

The net present value is ☐ ▼

Picklist:

Positive
Negative

....

Task 14.4

A Ltd is thinking of investing in Project B.

(a) **Complete the table below to calculate the net present value of Project B, rounding to the nearest whole £. You MUST use minus signs where appropriate.**

	Year 0 £	Year 1 £	Year 2 £	Year 3 £	Year 4 £
Net cash flows	-180,000	42,000	50,000	75,000	80,000
PV factors (15%)	1.000	0.8696	0.7561	0.6575	0.5718
Discounted cash flow					
NPV					

(b) **Project B is also to be evaluated using a cost of capital of 10%.**

Complete the table below to calculate the net present value of Project B, rounding to the nearest whole £. You MUST use minus signs where appropriate.

	Year 0 £	Year 1 £	Year 2 £	Year 3 £	Year 4 £
Net cash flows	-180,000	42,000	50,000	75,000	80,000
PV factors (10%)	1.000	0.9090	0.8264	0.7513	0.6830
Discounted cash flow					
NPV					

(c) **What is the approximate internal rate of return (IRR) of the project?**

☐ 0%

☐ 10%

☐ 12.5%

☐ 15%

Task 14.5

A project has the following NPVs at various costs of capital.

Cost of capital	NPV £
7%	20,255
9%	12,515
11%	5,395

What is the approximate IRR of the project?

☐ 0%

☐ 7.4%

☐ 10%

☐ 11.4%

Task 14.6

A project has the following NPVs at the following discount rates.

Discount rate %	NPV £
12	6,000
14	-3,000

What is the approximate IRR of the project?

☐ 1.3%

☐ 12.7%

☐ 13.3%

☐ 16.0%

Answer bank

Answer bank

Costs and Revenues Answer bank

Chapter 1

Task 1.1

	Financial accounting	Management accounting
Users	External to the organisation	Internal management
Timing	Annual	When required
Type of information	Historic	Historic and future
Format	Specified by law	To be useful

Task 1.2

```
COST CARD
                                          £
Direct Materials                          X
Direct labour                             X
Direct expenses                           X
Prime cost                                X
Production overheads                      X
Production cost                           X
Non-production overheads
    – selling and distribution            X
    – administration                      X
    – finance                             X
Total cost                                X
```

Task 1.3

The correct answer is: A maintenance assistant in a factory maintenance department.

The maintenance assistant is not working directly on the organisation's output but is performing an indirect task. All the other three options describe tasks that involve working directly on the output.

Task 1.4

The correct answer is: Costs and revenues

Profit centre managers are normally responsible for costs and revenues only.

....

Task 1.5

The correct answer is: Staples to fix the fabric to the seat of a chair

Indirect costs are those which **cannot be easily identified** with a specific cost unit. Although the staples could probably be identified with a specific chair, the cost is likely to be relatively insignificant. The expense of tracing such costs does not usually justify the possible benefits from calculating more accurate direct costs. The cost of the staples would therefore be treated as an indirect cost, to be included as a part of the overhead absorption rate.

The other options all represent significant costs which can be traced to a specific cost unit. Therefore they are classified as direct costs.

....

Task 1.6

The correct answer is: The total of direct costs

Prime cost is the total of direct material, direct labour and direct expenses.

All costs incurred in manufacturing a product describes total production cost, including absorbed production overhead. **The material cost of a product** is only a part of prime cost.

....

Task 1.7

COST CARD – TOY SOLDIER	
	£
Direct materials — Wood and paint	3.50
Direct labour — Toy maker's wages	3.00
Direct expenses — Hire of special tools	0.50
Prime cost	7.00
Rent, rates, heat and light	0.30
Production cost	7.30
Non-production overheads:	
Advertising and sales promotion	0.70
Total cost	8.00

Task 1.8

The correct answer is: A branch of a high street retailer. A cost object is any activity for which a separate measurement of costs is desired. Examples include the cost of a product, the cost of operating a department and the cost of a service.

Task 1.9

The correct answer is: A selling and distribution overhead. The deliveries occur after a sale is made, therefore drivers' wages are a selling and distribution overhead.

Task 1.10

	Drag and drop choice
Carbon for racquet heads	Direct material
Office stationery	Administration costs
Wages of employees stringing racquets	Direct labour
Supervisors' salaries	Indirect labour
Advertising stand at badminton tournaments	Selling and distribution costs

Chapter 2

Task 2.1

Cost types	
Production cost	**Factory heat and light, Depreciation of plant and machinery**
Selling and distribution cost	**Sales Director's salary, Depreciation of delivery vans, Fuel and oil for delivery vans**
Administration cost	**Finance Director's salary**

Task 2.2

Graph A – variable cost per unit

Graph B – total fixed cost across level of activity

Task 2.3

	Output (units)	Total cost £
Highest	26,500	410,000
Lowest	16,000	252,500
Increase	10,500	157,500

Variable cost per unit = 157,500/10,500 = £15 per unit

Fixed cost

16,000 × £15	= £240,000
£252,500 – £240,000	= £12,500
OR	
26,500 × £15	= £397,500
£410,000 – £397,500	= £12,500

Task 2.4

The correct answer is Graph 2. Graph 2 shows that costs increase in line with activity levels.

Task 2.5

The correct answer is Graph 1. Graph 1 shows that fixed costs remain the same whatever the level of activity.

Task 2.6

The correct answer is Graph 1. Graph 1 shows that cost per unit remains the same at different levels of activity.

Task 2.7

The correct answer is Graph 4. Graph 4 shows that semi-variable costs have a fixed element and a variable element.

Task 2.8

The correct answer is Graph 3. Graph 3 shows that the step fixed costs go up in 'steps' as the level of activity increases.

Task 2.9

The correct answer is: £5,100

	Units	£
High output	1,100	18,300
Low output	700	13,500
Variable cost	400	4,800

Variable cost per unit £4,800/£400 = £12 per unit

Fixed costs = £18,300 − (£12 × 1,100) = £5,100

Therefore the correct answer is £5,100.

£13,500 is the total cost for an activity of 700 units

£13,200 is the total variable cost for 1,100 units (1,100 × £12)

£4,800 is the difference between the costs incurred at the two activity levels recorded

Task 2.10

The correct answer is variable. In the long run, all costs are variable.

....

Task 2.11

The correct answer is: £76,000

	£
Variable costs 8,000 × £8	64,000
Fixed costs	12,000
	76,000

....

Chapter 3

Task 3.1

(a) The EOQ is 600 kg = $\sqrt{\dfrac{[2 \times 90,000 \times 2]}{1}}$

(b) and (c) **Inventory record card – FIFO**

Date	Receipts Quantity kg	Receipts Cost per kg (£)	Receipts Total cost (£)	Issues Quantity kg	Issues Cost per kg (£)	Issues Total cost (£)	Balance Quantity kg	Balance Total cost (£)
Balance as at 22 September							150	180
24 September	600	1.398	839				750	1,019
26 September				400	1.325	530	350	489
28 September	600	1.402	841				950	1,330
30 September				500	1.398	699	450	631

Note that the cost of the 400 kg issued on 26 September is made up of

  150 kg @ £1.20 = £180

  250 kg @ £1.398 = £350

Total   400 kg = £530   So the cost per kg = £530 ÷ 400 kg = 1.325

Note that the cost of the 500 kg issued on 30 September is made up of

  350 kg @ £1.398 = £489

  150 kg @ £1.402 = £210

Total   500 kg = £699   So the cost per kg = £699 ÷ 500 kg = 1.398

Task 3.2

Inventory record card

Date	Receipts			Issues			Balance	
	Quantity kg	Cost per kg (£)	Total cost (£)	Quantity kg	Cost per kg (£)	Total cost (£)	Quantity kg	Total cost (£)
Balance as at 1 January							4,000	10,000
31 January	1,000	2.0	2,000				5,000	12,000
15 February				3,000	2.5	7,500	2,000	4,500
28 February	1,500	2.5	3,750				3,500	8,250
14 March				500	2.5	1,250	3,000	7,000

Task 3.3

Inventory record card – AVCO

Inventory Record Card								
Date	Purchases			Requisitions			Balance	
	Quantity (kg)	Cost £	Total cost £	Quantity	Cost £	Total cost £	Quantity	Total cost £
1 Jan							300	7,500
2 Jan				250	25.00	6,250	50	1,250
12 Jan	400	25.75	10,300				450	11,550
21 Jan				200	25.67	5,134	250	6,416
29 Jan				75	25.66	1,925	175	4,491

Task 3.4

Date	Receipts			Issues			Balance	
	Quantity kg	Cost per kg (£)	Total cost (£)	Quantity kg	Cost per kg (£)	Total cost (£)	Quantity kg	Total cost (£)
1 January	4,000	2.50	10,000				4,000	10,000
31 January	1,000	2.00	2,000				5,000	12,000
15 February				3,000	2.50	7,500	2,000	4,500
28 February	1,500	2.50	3,750				3,500	8,250
14 March				500	2.50	1,250	3,000	7,000

Task 3.5

Date	Receipts			Issues			Balance	
	Quantity kg	Cost per kg (£)	Total cost (£)	Quantity kg	Cost per kg (£)	Total cost (£)	Quantity kg	Total cost (£)
1 January	4,000	2.50	10,000				4,000	10,000
31 January	1,000	2.00	2,000				5,000	12,000
15 February				3,000	2.33	7,000	2,000	5,000
28 February	1,500	2.50	3,750				3,500	8,750
14 March				500	2.50	1,250	3,000	7,500

Note that the cost of the 3,000 kg issued on 15 February is made up of

$\quad$ 1,000 kg @ £2.00 = £2,000

$\quad$ <u>2,000</u> kg @ £2.50 = <u>£5,000</u>

Total $\quad$ 3,000 kg $\qquad$ = £7,000

So the cost per kg = £7,000 ÷ 3,000 kg = £2.33 and this gives a rounding difference in the table above because 3,000kg × £2.33 = £6,990 rather than £7,000.

· ·

Task 3.6

The economic order quantity is $\boxed{300}$ units.

The formula for the economic order quantity (EOQ) is

$$EOQ = \sqrt{\frac{2cd}{h}}$$

With

c $\qquad$ = £10

d $\qquad$ = 5,400

h $\qquad$ = £0.10 × 12 months = £1.20

$$EOQ = \sqrt{\frac{2 \times £10 \times 5,400}{£1.20}}$$

$$= \sqrt{90,000}$$

$$= 300 \text{ units}$$

· ·

Task 3.7

The economic order quantity is $\boxed{175}$ units (to the nearest whole unit).

$$EOQ = \sqrt{\frac{2cd}{h}}$$

$$= \sqrt{\frac{2 \times £100 \times 1,225}{£8}}$$

$$= \sqrt{30,625}$$

$$= 175 \text{ units}$$

· ·

Task 3.8

The maximum inventory level was $\boxed{6,180}$ units

Reorder level = maximum usage × maximum lead time

= 130 × 26 = 3,380 units

Maximum level = reorder level + reorder quantity − (minimum usage × minimum lead time)

= 3,380 + 4,000 − (60 × 20)

= 6,180 units.

Chapter 4

Task 4.1

Employee's weekly timesheet for week ending 14 May

Employee: H. Hector			Cost Centre: Lipsy calibration			
Employee number: LP100			Basic pay per hour: £9.00			
	Hours spent on production	Hours worked on indirect work	Notes	Basic pay £	Overtime premium £	Total pay £
Monday	6	1	10am-11am setting up of machinery	63	0	63
Tuesday	3	4	9am-1pm department meeting	63	0	63
Wednesday	8			72	3	75
Thursday	8			72	3	75
Friday	6	1	3pm-4pm health and safety training	63	0	63
Saturday	4			36	9	45
Sunday	4			36	36	72
Total	39	6		405	51	456

Task 4.2

Employee's weekly timesheet for week ending 14 May

Employee: H. Hector			Cost Centre: Lipsy calibration		
Employee number: LP100			Basic pay per hour: £10.00		

	Hours spent on production	Hours worked on indirect work	Notes	Basic pay £	Overtime premium £	Total pay £
Monday	6	1	10am-11am setting up of machinery	70	0	70
Tuesday	3	4	9am-1pm department meeting	70	0	70
Wednesday	8			80	2.50	82.50
Thursday	8			80	2.50	82.50
Friday	6	1	3pm-4pm health and safety training	70	0	70
Saturday	4			40	0	40
Sunday	4			40	20	60
Total	**39**	**6**		450	25	475

Task 4.3

These details are recorded in the wages control account as follows:

Wages control account

	£		£
Bank	250,000	WIP	275,000
HM Revenue & Customs	62,500	Production overhead control	75,000
Welfare scheme			
Contributions	37,500		
	350,000		350,000

Task 4.4

Work in progress control account

		£		£
31 May	Wages control	275,000		

Production overhead control

		£		£
31 May	Wages control	75,000		

··

Task 4.5

The correct answer is: Maintenance workers in a shoe factory. Maintenance workers will not be involved in actually making the shoes. Machinists in a clothes manufacturer will be involved in making the clothes and are therefore direct labour. Bricklayers actually make the buildings so are also direct labour.

··

Task 4.6

✓ DEBIT Overhead control CREDIT Wages control

Indirect wages are 'collected' in the overhead control account, for subsequent absorption into work in progress.

··

Task 4.7

	Code	Dr £	Cr £
Manufacturing department A wages	2300	18,500	
Manufacturing department A wages	6000		18,500
Manufacturing department B wages	2400	22,500	
Manufacturing department B wages	6000		22,500
Maintenance department wages	3400	12,700	
Maintenance department wages	6000		12,700
General admin department salaries	3500	7,600	
General admin department salaries	6000		7,600

··

Task 4.8

✓ DEBIT   Work-in-progress account   CREDIT   Wages control

The **direct costs of production**, of which direct wages are a part, are **debited to the work in progress account**. The credit entry is made in the **wages control account**, where the wages cost has been 'collected' **prior to its analysis** between direct and indirect wages.

●●●

Task 4.9

(a) **Employee's weekly timesheet for week ending 7 December**

	Hours	Total pay £
Basic pay (including basic hours for overtime)	48	720.00
Mon-Fri overtime premium	7	52.50
Sat-Sun overtime premium	6	90.00
Total		862.50

(b)   £135

   £15 × 30% = £4.50 per unit

   30 extra units × £4.50 = £135

(c)   4,200   units

   7,000 units × 60% = 4,200 units

●●●

Task 4.10

£0.325

$$\frac{£13,650}{42,000} = £0.325$$

●●●

Chapter 5

Task 5.1

(a) The correct answer is: Silicon moulding £51/hour, Silicon extrusion £56/hour

(b) The correct answer is: Silicon moulding £18/hour, Silicon extrusion £17/hour

(c) The correct answer is: Silicon moulding over-absorbed £24,201, Silicon extrusion under-absorbed £1,896

Task 5.2

	Silicon moulding	Silicon extrusion
Budgeted overheads (£)	450,000	352,520
Budgeted direct labour hours	22,500	17,626
Budgeted machine hours	8,182	6,409

Task 5.3
(a)

	Silicon moulding	Silicon extrusion
Actual direct labour hours	21,222	17,144
Actual machine hours	8,459	6,501
Budgeted overhead absorbed – labour hrs	424,440	342,880
Budgeted overhead absorbed – machine hrs	465,245	357,555

(b)

	Silicon moulding	Silicon extrusion
Actual overheads (£)	425,799	354,416
Difference – labour hrs	1,359	11,536
Difference – machine hrs	39,446	3,139

Task 5.4

The correct answer is: Absorbed overheads exceed actual overheads.

Absorbed overheads exceeding budgeted overheads could lead to under-absorbed overheads if actual overheads far exceeded both budgeted overheads and the overhead absorbed. Actual overheads exceeding budgeted overheads could lead to under-absorbed overheads if overhead absorbed does not increase in line with actual overhead incurred.

Task 5.5

The correct answer is: £405,000

Budgeted absorption rate for fixed overhead	= £360,000/8,000
	= £45 per hour
Fixed overhead absorbed	= 9,000 hours × £45
	= £405,000

If you selected £384,000 you based your absorption calculations on sales units instead of labour hours.

If you selected £432,000 you calculated the correct figure for fixed overhead absorbed but also added the variable overheads.

£459,000 is the figure for actual total overhead incurred.

Task 5.6

The correct answer is: under-absorbed by £27,000

Actual fixed overhead incurred	= £432,000
Fixed overhead absorbed	= £405,000 (from Task 5.5)
Fixed overhead under absorbed	= £27,000

If you selected under-absorbed by £72,000, you simply calculated the difference between the budgeted and actual fixed overhead. If you selected under-absorbed by £75,000, you based your absorption calculations on sales units instead of production units. If you selected over-absorbed by £27,000 you performed the calculations correctly but misinterpreted the result as an over absorption.

Chapter 6

Task 6.1

	Basis of apportionment	Silicon moulding £	Silicon extrusion £	Maintenance £	Stores £	General Admin £	Totals £
Depreciation of plant and equipment	NBV of plant and equipment	904,669	1,105,706				2,010,375
Power for production machinery	Production machinery power usage (KwH)	572,500	1,215,000				1,787,500
Rent and rates	Floor space			74,648	93,310	93,310	261,268
Light and heat	Floor space			16,500	20,625	20,625	57,750
Indirect labour	Allocated			253,750	90,125	600,251	944,126
Totals		1,477,169	2,320,706	344,898	204,060	714,186	5,061,019
Reapportion Maintenance		120,714	224,184	(344,898)			
Reapportion Stores		81,624	122,436		(204,060)		
Reapportion General Admin		357,093	357,093			(714,186)	
Total overheads to production centres		2,036,600	3,024,419				5,061,019

Task 6.2

(a)

	Basis of apportionment	Silicon moulding £	Silicon extrusion £	Maintenance £	Stores £	General Admin £	Totals £
Depreciation of plant and equipment	Headcount	972,762	1,037,613				2,010,375
Power for production machinery	Headcount	864,919	922,581				1,787,500
Rent and rates	Floor space			74,648	93,310	93,310	261,268
Light and heat	Floor space			16,500	20,625	20,625	57,750
Indirect labour	Allocated			253,750	90,125	600,251	944,126
Totals		1,837,681	1,960,194	344,898	204,060	714,176	5,061,019
Reapportion Maintenance		120,714	224,184	(344,898)			
Reapportion Stores		81,624	122,436		(204,060)		
Reapportion General Admin		464,221	249,965			(714,186)	
Total overheads to production centres		2,504,240	2,556,779				5,061,019

(b) The manager would most likely argue with the revised basis of allocation as his/her costs have increased by £467,640. The use of headcount to apportion machinery costs is not common and the manager could argue that depreciation based on NBV, and power on consumption are better bases for reapportioning these costs. Nonetheless, if the cost centre is using more general admin then it is fair that it should bear more of that cost.

Task 6.3

£16.50

The full absorption cost of a unit of Em excludes the fixed administration, selling and distribution costs.

£18.20 – £1.70 = £16.50

Chapter 7

Task 7.1

Service	Cost unit
Road, rail and air transport services	Passenger/kilometre, tonne/kilometre
Hotels	Occupied bed-night
Education	Full-time student
Hospitals	Patient-day
Catering establishments	Meal served

Task 7.2

Job number 03456

	Budget £	Actual £	Variance F/A £
Direct materials			
Plasterboard	3,600.00	3,500.00	100F
Wood & door frames	4,750.00	4,802.00	52A
Insulation	1,050.00	1,145.00	95A
Electrical fittings	320.00	300.00	20F
Windows	2,220.00	2,576.00	356A
Paint	270.00	250.00	20F
Direct labour			
Construction	554.00	641.00	87A
Electrical	224.00	160.00	64F
Decorating	165.00	205.00	40A
Direct expenses			
Hire of specialist lathe	240.00	240.00	0
Overheads (based upon direct labour hours)			
84/90 hours @ £15.00	1,260.00	1,350.00	90A

Task 7.3

(a) and (b)

	Budget £	Actual £	Variance F/A £	%
Direct materials				
Plasterboard	3,600.00	3,500.00	100F	2.8
Wood & door frames	4,750.00	4,802.00	52A	1.1
Insulation	1,050.00	1,145.00	95A	9.0
Electrical fittings	320.00	300.00	20F	6.3
Windows	2,220.00	2,576.00	356A	16.0
Paint	270.00	250.00	20F	7.4
Direct labour				
Construction	554.00	641.00	87A	15.7
Electrical	224.00	160.00	64F	28.6
Decorating	165.00	205.00	40A	24.2
Direct expenses				
Hire of specialist lathe	240.00	240.00	0	0
Overheads (based upon direct labour hours)				
84/90 hours @ £15.00	1,260.00	1,350.00	90A	7.1
Total cost	14,653.00	15,169.00	516.00 A	
Profit	2,930.60	2,414.60		
Net price	17,583.60	17,583.60		
VAT at 20%	3,516.72	3,516.72		
Total price	21,100.32	21,100.32		

(c) (2,930.60 – 2,414.60)/2,930.60 = 17.6%

Task 7.4

☑ High levels of indirect costs as a proportion of total cost

☑ Cost units are often intangible

☑ Use of composite cost units

In service costing it is difficult to identify many attributable direct costs. Many costs must be treated as indirect costs and shared over several cost units, therefore there are high levels of indirect costs as a proportion of total cost. Many services are intangible, for example a haircut or a cleaning service provide no physical, tangible product. Composite cost units such as passenger-mile or bed-night are often used in service costing. 'Use of equivalent units' does not apply because equivalent units are more often used in costing for tangible products.

Task 7.5

(a)   ☐ £18.20

$$\frac{582,400}{32,000} = £18.20$$

(b)   ☐ £16.50

$$\frac{582,400 - 54,400}{32,000} = £16.50$$

(c)   ☐ £528,000

£16.50 × 32,000 units = £528,000 or £582,400 − £54,400 = £528,000

Chapter 8

Task 8.1

(a)

Description	Kg	Unit cost £	Total cost £	Description	Kg	Unit cost £	Total cost £
Material TL4	700	1.35	945	Normal loss	145	0.60	87
Material TL3	350	1.50	525	Output	1,305	6.66	8,691
Material TL9	400	1.25	500				
Labour			3,700				
Overheads			3,108				
	1,450		8,778		1,450		8,778

(b)

	Debit	Credit
Abnormal loss account	✓	
Process account		✓

Task 8.2

Description	Kg	Unit cost £	Total cost £	Description	Kg	Unit cost £	Total cost £
Material TL4	700	1.35	945	Normal loss	290	0.60	174
Material TL3	350	1.50	525	Output	1,160	7.07	8,196*
Material TL9	400	1.25	500				
Labour			3,040				
Overheads			3,360				
	1,450		8,370		1,450		8,370

* Note there is a rounding difference here.

The decision made to employ cheaper employees has resulted in the process costing more but higher losses are incurred too. However over time, the workers may get more efficient, taking less time and the losses may go down.

Task 8.3

The correct answer is 2,000 kg

Process account

	Dr		Cr
Opening WIP	4,500	Output	60,400
Input	54,300	Normal loss	400
Abnormal gain	2,000		–
	60,800		60,800

The abnormal gain is the balancing figure. 60,800 – 4,500 – 54,300 = 2,000

Task 8.4

The quantity of good production achieved was ⟨2,625⟩ kg.

Good production = input – normal loss – abnormal loss

$$= 3,000 - (10\% \times 3,000) - 75$$
$$= 3,000 - 300 - 75$$
$$= \underline{2,625} \text{ kg}$$

Task 8.5

(a) The value credited to the process account for the scrap value of the normal loss for the period will be £ ⎡ 100 ⎤ (to the nearest £).

Normal loss = 10% × input

= 10% × 5,000 kg

= 500 kg

When scrap has a value, normal loss is valued at the value of the scrap ie 20p per kg.

Normal loss = £0.20 × 500 kg

= £100

(b) The amount of abnormal loss for the period is 300 kg.

	Kg
Input	5,000
Normal loss (10% × 5,000 kg)	(500)
Abnormal loss	(300)
Output	4,200

Task 8.6

(a) B An equivalent unit calculation is used in process costing to value any incomplete units within work in progress and losses.

Option A describes the output from any process, where all completed units are identical.

Option C describes a cost unit, and Option D describes a standard hour.

Task 8.7

We use equivalent units.

	Equivalent units
Completed production	20,400
Work in progress (8,000 × 25%)	2,000
	22,400

Therefore during the period the equivalent of 22,400 completed units have passed through the process. The cost per equivalent unit (EU) can now be found.

$$\text{Cost per equivalent unit} = \frac{£56,000}{22,400 \text{ EU}}$$

= £2.50 per equivalent unit

Task 8.8

(a)

	Units	Materials Proportion complete	Equivalent units	Labour/overheads Proportion complete	Equivalent units
Completed	8,300	100%	8,300	100%	8,300
Work in progress	1,000	70%	700	60%	600
Total equivalent units			9,000		8,900
Cost per equivalent unit		=	£21,600	=	£13,350
			9,000		8,900
			= £2.40 per EU		= £1.50 per EU

(b)

	£
Completed output	
Materials (8,300 × £2.40)	19,920
Labour/overhead (8,300 × £1.50)	12,450
	32,370
Work in progress	
Materials (700 × £2.40)	1,680
Labour/overhead (600 × £1.50)	900
	2,580

··

Task 8.9

(a) **FIFO**

Unit calculation:

Opening + Input = Good output + Closing WIP
WIP   Units

	Actual Units	Materials	Equivalent Units Labour	Overheads
Opening WIP W1	100	–	40	70
Goods started and finished	3,940	3,940	3,940	3,940
(= output – opening WIP)				
Good output	4,040	3,940	3,980	4,010
Closing WIP W2	160	160	96	96
Equivalent units	4,200	4,100	4,076	4,106

Workings

1   Opening WIP is 100% complete for materials but 60% for labour and 30% for overheads.

     To complete   –   Labour $(100 - 60)\% = 40\% \times 100 = 40$

                –   Overheads $(100 - 30)\% = 70\% \times 100 = 70$

2   Closing WIP   –   100% complete for materials so 100% × 160 = 160

–   60% complete for labour so 60% × 160 = 96

–   60% complete for overheads so 60% × 160 = 96

(b) **Statement of cost per equivalent unit**

	£	£	£
Input costs	45,100	32,608	16,424
Cost per equivalent unit	11.00	8.00	4.00
= Input costs/Equivalent units			

(c) **Value of units**

		£
Value of good output =	Costs b/f in opening WIP =	1,220
	Materials 3,940 × £11	43,340
	Labour 3,980 × £8	31,840
	Overheads 4,010 × £4	16,040
		92,440

Value of Closing WIP = 160 × £11 + 96 × £8 + 96 × £4 = £2,912

(d) **Process account**

Process

	Units	£		Units	£
Opening WIP b/f	100	1,220	Good output	4,040	92,440
Raw Materials	4,100	45,100	(see st of equiv units)		
Labour		32,608	Closing WIP W2	160	2,912
Overheads		16,424			
	4,200	95,352		4,200	95,352

Task 8.10

(a) **Statement of equivalent units**

	Actual units	Materials	Equivalent units Labour	Overheads
Good output	4,040	4,040	4,040	4,040
Closing WIP	160	160	96	96
Equivalent units	4,200	4,200	4,136	4,136

(b) **Costs**

	£	£	£
Costs b/f (£1,220) (from the example)	800	360	60
Input costs	45,100	32,608	16,424
	45,900	32,968	16,484
Cost per equivalent unit = Input costs/Equivalent units	10.93	7.97	3.99

Total £22.89

(c) **Value of units**

Value of good output = £22.89 × 4,040 = £92,476

Value of Closing WIP = 160 × £10.93 + 96 × £7.97 + 96 × £3.99 = £2,897

(d) **Process account**

Process

	Units	£		Units	£
Opening WIP b/f	100	1,220	Output	4,040	92,476
Raw Materials	4,100	45,100	Closing WIP c/d	160	2,897
Labour		32,608			
Overheads		16,424	Rounding		(21)
	4,200	95,352		4,200	95,352

Chapter 9

Task 9.1

Batches produced and sold	3,000	3,750	5,000
	£	£	£
Sales revenue	60,000	75,000	100,000
Variable costs:			
• Direct materials 1.90	5,700	7,125	9,500
• Direct labour 9	27,000	33,750	45,000
• Overheads 3.1	9,300	11,625	15,500
Semi-variable costs:	9,450		
• Variable element		7,500	10,000
• Fixed element		3,450	3,450
Total cost	51,450	63,450	83,450
Total profit	8,550	11,550	16,550
Profit per batch (to 2 decimal places)	2.85	3.08	3.31

Workings

Sales revenue   £60,000 / 3,000 batches = £20 per batch

Direct materials   £5,700 / 3,000 batches = £1.90 per batch

Direct labour   £27,000 / 3,000 batches = £9 per batch

Variable overheads   £9,300 / 3,000 batches = £3.1 per batch

(Note that the overheads are variable and therefore we calculate a cost per batch. If they were fixed overheads then the cost would be the same for 3,000 batches, 3,750 batches and 5,000 batches.)

Semi-variable cost

7,500	£18,450
7,000	£ 9,450
500	9,000

Variable cost = £9,000 / 500 = £2 per batch

Fixed cost = £18,450 – (7,500 × £2) = £3,450

···

Task 9.2

(a)

Batches produced and sold	3,000	3,750	5,000
	£	£	£
Sales revenue	60,000	75,000	100,000
Variable costs:			
• Direct materials 2	6,000	7,500	10,000
• Direct labour 10	30,000	37,500	50,000
• Overheads 3.2	9,600	12,000	16,000
Semi-variable costs:	9,450		
• Variable element		7,500	10,000
• Fixed element		3,450	3,450
Total cost	55,050	67,950	89,450
Total profit	4,950	7,050	10,550
Profit per batch (to 2 decimal places)	1.65	1.88	2.11

···

Task 9.3

Batches produced and sold	3,000	4,000
	£	£
Sales revenue	60,000	80,000
Variable costs:		
• Direct materials	6,000	8,000
• Direct labour	30,000	40,000
• Overheads	9,600	12,800
Semi-variable costs:		
• Variable element	6,000	8,000
• Fixed element	3,450	3,450
Total cost	55,050	72,250
Total profit	4,950	7,750
Profit per batch (to 2 decimal places)	1.65	1.94

Reject.

The profit per batch is less than £2 at 4,000 batches, so management should reject the order.

....

Chapter 10

Task 10.1

	Flexed Budget	Actual	Variance	Favourable F or Adverse A
Volume sold	156,000	156,000		
	£'000	£'000	£'000	
Sales revenue	1,248	1,326	78	F
Less costs:				
Direct materials	390	372	18	F
Direct labour	468	444	24	F
Overheads	225	250	25	A
Operating profit	165	260	95	F

Task 10.2

	Flexed Budget	Actual	Budget unit cost/revenue	Actual unit cost/revenue
Volume sold	156,000	156,000		
	£'000	£'000		
Sales revenue	1,248	1,326	8	8.50
Less costs:				
Direct materials	390	372	2.50	2.38
Direct labour	468	444	3	2.85
Overheads	225	250		
Operating profit	165	260	1.06	1.67

They are all true. The unit selling price is higher than budgeted, which may be due to a rise in the sales price not planned for in the budget, or fewer bulk discounts to customers if these were planned for. The lower unit price for materials may arise from bulk buying discounts or new cheaper sources of supply. The lower labour costs may be due to a change in the make up of employees so there are more lower paid employees, or efficiency savings so fewer employees make the same number of SHEPs.

Chapter 11

Task 11.1

Production overheads absorbed into production	Debit: WIP	Credit: Production overheads
Indirect labour transferred to production overheads	Debit: Production overheads	Credit: Wages
Completed WIP transferred to finished goods	Debit: Finished goods	Credit: WIP
Direct materials issued to production	Debit: WIP	Credit: Materials

Task 11.2

	Drag and drop choice
Transaction 1	Debit: production overheads, Credit: statement of profit or loss
Transaction 2	Debit: statement of profit or loss, Credit: production overheads

Task 11.3

The correct answer is: Debit Production overhead control account Credit Materials control account

The cost of indirect materials issued is credited to the materials control account and 'collected' in the production overhead control account pending its absorption into work in progress.

Debit WIP account and Credit Materials control account represents the entries for the issue to production of **direct materials**.

Debit Cost of sales and Credit Materials control account is not correct. The issue of materials should not be charged direct to cost of sales. The cost of materials issued should first be analysed as direct or indirect and charged to work in progress or the overhead control account accordingly.

Chapter 12

Task 12.1

(a) **Absorption costing – unit cost**

	£
Direct materials	8.50
Direct labour	17.00
Variable overheads	3.00
Prime cost	28.50
Fixed overheads ((£850,000/250,000) × 2)	6.80
Absorption cost	35.30

(b) **Marginal costing – unit cost**

	£
Direct materials	8.50
Direct labour	17.00
Variable overheads	3.00
Prime cost or marginal cost	28.50

Task 12.2

In the long run, total profit for a company will be the same for both types of costing whether marginal costing or absorption costing is used.

Task 12.3

It might be argued that absorption costing is preferable to marginal costing **in management accounting,** in order to be consistent with the requirement of current accounting standards and financial reporting.

Task 12.4

(a) £45,400

		£	£
Sales	(5,200 × £30)		156,000
Direct materials	(5,800 × £6)	34,800	
Direct labour	(5,800 × £7.50)	43,500	
Variable overhead	(5,800 × £2.50)	14,500	
		92,800	
Less closing inventory	(600 × £16)	9,600	
			(83,200)
Contribution			72,800
Less fixed costs			27,400
			45,400

(b) £48,400

		£	£
Sales	(5,200 × £30)		156,000
Materials	(5,800 × £6)	34,800	
Labour	(5,800 × £7.50)	43,500	
Variable overhead	(5,800 × £2.50)	14,500	
Fixed costs	(5,800 × £5)	29,000	
Less closing inventories	(600 × £21)	(12,600)	
			(109,200)
Over-absorbed overhead (W)			1,600
Absorption costing profit			48,400

Working		£
Overhead absorbed	(5,800 × £5)	29,000
Overhead incurred		27,400
Over-absorbed overhead		1,600

Task 12.5

(a) $\boxed{£36.40}$

$$\frac{£582,400}{16,000} = £36.40$$

(b) $\boxed{£33.00}$

$$\frac{£582,400 - £54,400}{16,000} = £33.00$$

(c) $\boxed{£528,000}$

£33.00 × 16,000 units = £528,000 (or £582,400 – £54,400 = £528,000)

(d) $\boxed{£454,400}$

£176,000 + £230,400 + £48,000 = £454,400

(e) $\boxed{£28.40}$

$$\frac{£454,400}{16,000} = £28.40$$

Chapter 13

Task 13.1

(a) | 9,000 units | Breakeven point in units = Fixed costs / contribution per unit

= £45,000 / (£22 − £17)

= 9,000 units

(b) | £198,000 | Breakeven point in units × selling price per unit

= 9,000 × £22

= £198,000

(c)

Units of COLIN sold	9,500	10,500
	£	£
Margin of safety (units)	500	1,500
Margin of safety percentage	$\left(\dfrac{500}{9,500} \times 100\%\right) =$ **5%**	$\left(\dfrac{1,500}{10,500} \times 100\%\right) =$ **14%**
Margin of safety revenue (units × sales price)	11,000	33,000

(d) | 13,000 units | Activity level $= \dfrac{\text{Fixed costs} + \text{target profit}}{\text{Contribution per unit}} = \dfrac{45,000 + 20,000}{5}$

= 13,000 units

(e) The correct answer is: the breakeven point will decrease and the margin of safety will increase

Task 13.2

(a) 8,000 × £(22 − 17) = £40,000

(b) | £132,000 | which is (£30,000/£5 × £22) or (6,000 × £22)

(c)

Units of COLIN sold	6,500	7,000
	£	£
Margin of safety (units)	500	1,000
Margin of safety percentage	$\left(\dfrac{500}{6,500} \times 100\%\right) =$ 8%	$\left(\dfrac{1,000}{7,000} \times 100\%\right) =$ 14%

(d) [8,000 units] Yes as it is at the maximum level of production.

Task 13.3

The correct answer is 3,000 units

$$\text{Breakeven point} = \frac{\text{Fixed costs}}{\text{Contribution per unit}} = \frac{£30,000}{£(15-5)} = 3,000 \text{ units}$$

If you selected 2,000 units you divided the fixed cost by the selling price, but remember that the selling price also has to cover the variable cost. 4,000 units is the margin of safety, and if you selected 6,000 units, you divided the fixed cost by the variable cost per unit.

Task 13.4

The correct answer is: 20%

$$\text{Breakeven point} = \frac{\text{Fixed costs}}{\text{Contribution per unit}} = \frac{£96,000}{£(12-8)} = 24,000 \text{ units}$$

Budgeted sales   30,000 units

Margin of safety   6,000 units

$$\text{Expressed as a \% of budget} = \frac{6,000}{30,000} \times 100\% = 20\%$$

If you selected 25% you calculated the correct margin of safety in units, but you then expressed this as a percentage of the breakeven point. If you selected 73% you divided the fixed cost by the selling price to determine the breakeven point, but the selling price also has to cover the variable cost. You should have been able to eliminate 125% as an option; the margin of safety expressed as a percentage must always be less than 100 per cent.

Task 13.5

(a) The correct answer is: 10,090 units

$$\text{Breakeven point} = \frac{\text{Fixed costs}}{\text{Contribution per unit}}$$

$$= \frac{10,000 \times £(4.00 + 0.80)}{(£6.00 - (£1.20 + £0.40))}$$

$$= \frac{£48,000}{£4.40} = 10,909 \text{ units}$$

If you selected 8,000 units you divided the fixed cost by the selling price, but the selling price also has to cover the variable cost. 8,333 units ignores the selling costs, but these are costs that must be covered before the breakeven point is reached. 10,000 units is the budgeted sales volume, which happens to be below the breakeven point.

(b) The correct answer is: 13,409 units

Contribution required for target profit	= fixed costs + profit
	= £48,000 + £11,000
	= £59,000
÷ Contribution per unit (from part (a))	= £4.40
∴ Sales units required	= 13,409 units

If you selected 2,500 units you divided the required profit by the contribution per unit, but the fixed costs must be covered before any profit can be earned. If you selected 9,833 units you identified correctly the contribution required for the target profit, but you then divided by the selling price per unit instead of the contribution per unit. 10,625 units ignores the selling costs, which must be covered before a profit can be earned.

Chapter 14

Task 14.1

(a) The net present value is **Negative**.

	Year 0 £'000	Year 1 £'000	Year 2 £'000	Year 3 £'000	Year 4 £'000
Capital expenditure	(1,000)				
Sales income		350	400	400	350
Operating costs		(100)	(110)	(120)	(130)
Net cash flows	(1,000)	250	290	280	220
PV factors	1.0000	0.9009	0.8116	0.7312	0.6587
Discounted cash flows	(1,000)	225	235	205	145
Net present value	(190)				

(b) The payback period is **3** years and **10** months.

··

Task 14.2

£810,000. This is calculated as follows:

(all in £'000) 225 + 235 + 205 + 145 – capital expenditure = 0

Therefore capital expenditure = 810

··

Task 14.3

The net present value is **Positive**.

	Year 0 £'000	Year 1 £'000	Year 2 £'000	Year 3 £'000	Year 4 £'000
Capital expenditure	(810)				
Sales income		350	400	400	350
Operating costs		(100)	(110)	(120)	(130)
Net cash flows	(810)	250	290	280	220
PV factors	1.0000	0.9346	0.8734	0.8163	0.7629
Discounted cash flows	(810)	234	253	229	168
Net present value	74				

Task 14.4

(a)

	Year 0 £	Year 1 £	Year 2 £	Year 3 £	Year 4 £
Net cash flows	-180,000	42,000	50,000	75,000	80,000
PV factors (15%)	1.000	0.8696	0.7561	0.6575	0.5718
Discounted cash flow	-180,000	36,523	37,805	49,313	45,744
NPV	-10,615				

(b)

	Year 0 £	Year 1 £	Year 2 £	Year 3 £	Year 4 £
Net cash flows	-180,000	42,000	50,000	75,000	80,000
PV factors (10%)	1.000	0.9090	0.8264	0.7513	0.6830
Discounted cash flow	-180,000	38,178	41,320	56,348	54,640
NPV	10,486				

(c)   12.5%

At a cost of capital of 15% the NPV is negative. At a cost of capital of 10% the NPV is positive. So an NPV of zero must be somewhere in between 10% and 15%.

Task 14.5

11.4%

The IRR is the cost of capital which gives an NPV of zero. As you can see from the table, the higher the cost of capital, the closer the NPV is getting to zero. Therefore 11.4% is the correct answer.

Task 14.6

IRR = 13.3%

$$IRR = A + \left[\frac{a}{a-b} \times (B - A) \right]$$

$$IRR = 12 + \left[\frac{6,000}{6,000 - -3,000} \times (14 - 12) \right]$$

$$IRR = 12 + \left[\frac{6,000}{6,000 + 3,000} \times 2 \right]$$

$$\therefore IRR = 12 + \left[\frac{6,000}{9,000} \times 2 \right]$$

$$\therefore IRR = 13.3\%$$

AAT AQ2013 SAMPLE ASSESSMENT 1
COSTS AND REVENUES

Time allowed: 2½ hours

AAT AQ2013 SAMPLE ASSESSMENT 1

Task 1 (16 marks)

Broadsword Ltd had an opening balance of raw material PS99 on 1 December as shown below. During December it has made four transactions, for which the inventory record has only been partially updated. Broadsword uses the first in first out (FIFO) basis for inventory valuation in its internal management accounts.

(a) **Complete ALL entries in the inventory record (showing the cost per kilogram in £ to THREE decimal places), including balances at the end of each day. Only one entry is permitted per inventory record cell.**

Material PS99	Receipts			Issues			Balance	
Date	Quantity (kg)	Cost per kg (£)	Total cost (£)	Quantity (kg)	Cost per kg (£)	Total cost (£)	Quantity (kg)	Total cost (£)
Balance at 1 December							8,000	18,000
6 December	4,800		10,320					
13 December				7,200				
20 December	12,000	2,210						
27 December				4,800				

Broadsword is considering the effect of using the last in first out (LIFO) method of inventory valuation in its internal management accounts.

(b) **Complete the sentence below.**

Using the LIFO method, the issue of 7,200 kilograms to production on 13 December would be valued at a total of £ [   ].

Task 2 (16 marks)

Below are extracts from Broadsword Ltd's payroll for last week.

Date	Labour costs
10 December	Plastic extrusion manufacturing: production employees' pay £5,300
12 December	Plastic moulding manufacturing: production employees' pay £6,600
14 December	Stores department: employees' pay £1,400
16 December	General administration department: staff salaries £2,600

Complete the cost journal entries to record the four payroll payments made last week.

Date	Code		Dr (£)	Cr (£)
10 December		▼		
10 December		▼		
12 December		▼		
12 December		▼		
14 December		▼		
14 December		▼		
16 December		▼		
16 December		▼		

Drop-down list:

6400 Plastic extrusion direct costs
6500 Plastic moulding direct costs
7200 Operating overheads
8300 Non-operating overheads
5000 Wages control account

Task 3 (12 marks)

Some of Broadsword Ltd's employees working in its Plastic Moulding department work in teams.

Their basic hourly rate is £12.00 per hour and there are two rates of overtime as follows:

Overtime rate 1 – time and a quarter (basic rate plus an overtime premium equal to a quarter of basic pay)

Overtime rate 2 – time and a half (basic rate plus an overtime premium equal to half of basic pay)

Broadsword sets a target for production of every plastic component each month. A team bonus equal to 20% of basic hourly rate is payable for every equivalent unit of production in the month in excess of the target. The target for December was 20,000 units.

In December the production was 23,000 equivalent units.

All overtime and bonuses are included as part of the direct labour cost.

(a) **Complete the gaps in the table below to calculate the direct labour cost.**

Pay rate	Hours	£
Basic pay (including basic hours for overtime)	484	
Overtime premium rate 1	74	
Overtime premium rate 2	92	
Total cost before team bonus	650	
Bonus payment		
Total cost including team bonus		

(b) **Calculate the total direct labour cost per equivalent unit of the finished production for December. Give your answer in £s to FOUR decimal places.**

The direct labour cost per equivalent unit for December is £ [＿＿＿＿＿＿].

Broadsword has forecast the following information for the Plastic Moulding department for January:

The basic hourly rate will be increased to £12.50 per hour. The target for production is still 20,000 units and the bonus, equal to 20% of basic hourly rate, is still payable for equivalent units of production in excess of this.

18,400 units will be completed in January and the closing work in progress is expected to be 7,000 units which will be 80% complete with regard to labour. No opening work in progress was expected at the start of January.

(c) **Complete the following sentence by filling in the blanks.**

The equivalent units of production with regard to labour for January will be

[   ] and the bonus payable will be £ [   ].

Task 4 (18 marks)

Broadsword Ltd has the following information for its two profit centres and three cost centres:

Budgeted overheads	£	£
Depreciation charge for machinery		128,200
Variable machine running costs		96,100
Rents and rates of premises		24,300
Light, heat and power for premises		16,100
Indirect labour costs:		
Maintenance	15,200	
Stores	18,240	
General administration	20,900	
Total indirect labour cost		54,340

Additional information				
Department	Carrying amount of machinery (£)	Planned number of machine hours	Floor space (square metres)	Number of indirect employees
Profit centres:				
Plastic extrusion	780,000	17,952	12,600	14
Plastic moulding	420,000	8,448	12,600	12
Support department cost centres:				
Maintenance			4,200	3
Stores			8,400	3
General administration			4,200	3
Total	1,200,000	26,400	42,000	35

Overheads are allocated or apportioned on the most appropriate basis. The total overheads of the three support departments' cost centres are then reapportioned to the two profit centres using the direct method.

- 70% of the maintenance department's time is spent maintaining the machinery in the plastic extrusion profit centre and the remainder in the plastic moulding profit centre.

- The stores department makes 65% of its issues to the plastic extrusion profit centre and the remainder to the plastic moulding profit centre.

- General administration support costs can be split 50% to the plastic extrusion profit centre and 50% to the plastic moulding profit centre.

- There is no reciprocal servicing between the three support cost centres.

Use the following table to allocate or apportion the overheads using the most appropriate basis.

(Note: When reapportioning the service overheads, ensure that you enter totals both in the totals row and then again in the row appropriate to that service.)

	Basis of apportionment	Plastic extrusion £	Plastic moulding £	Maintenance £	Stores £	General administration £	Totals £
Depreciation charge for machinery	▼						
Variable machine running costs	▼						
Rent and rates of premises	▼						
Light, heat and power for premises	▼						
Indirect labour	▼						
Totals							
Reapportion Maintenance							
Reapportion Stores							
Reapportion General administration							
Total overheads to profit centres							

Drop-down list:

Allocated
Carrying amount of machinery
Floor space
Number of employees
Number of issues
Number of machine hours

Task 5 (15 marks)

Broadsword Ltd has prepared budgeted overheads and activity levels for Quarter 1 of next year.

The figures for its two production departments are as follows:

Quarter 1 budget	Plastic moulding	Plastic extrusion
Direct labour hours	5,784 hours	5,904 hours
Machine hours	1,800 hours	2,150 hours
Overheads	£130,140	£146,415

(a) **If both the plastic moulding department and the plastic extrusion department were heavily automated, what would the budgeted overhead absorption rate be for each department (to TWO decimal places)?**

Quarter 1 budget	Plastic moulding £	Plastic extrusion £
Budgeted overhead absorption rate	per hour	per hour

(b) **If both the plastic moulding department and the plastic extrusion department were labour intensive, what would the budgeted overhead absorption rate be for each department (to TWO decimal places)?**

Quarter 1 budget	Plastic moulding £	Plastic extrusion £
Budgeted overhead absorption rate	per hour	per hour

At the end of Quarter 1 it was found that actual overheads incurred in the plastic moulding department were £133,154. Overheads were recovered on a machine hours basis. The machine hours worked were 10% more than budgeted.

(c) **Complete the following sentence by selecting the appropriate response and inserting the correct amount.**

In Quarter 1 overheads for the plastic moulding department were [▼]

by £ [   ].

Drop-down list:

Under-absorbed
Over-absorbed

Task 6 (20 marks)

Broadsword Ltd has prepared budgeted information for three of its products, SW38, TX39 and UY40 for the next financial year.

Product	SW38	TX39	UY40
Sales revenue (£)	97,500	129,600	164,025
Direct materials (£)	31,500	43,200	54,675
Direct labour (£)	27,000	39,600	50,625

The company expects to produce and sell 15,000 units of SW38 and 18,000 units of TX39. The budgeted sales demand for UY40 is 35% greater than that of SW38. Budgeted total fixed costs are £44,525.

Complete the table below (to TWO decimal places) to show the budgeted contribution per unit of SW38, TX39 and UY40 sold, and the company's budgeted profit or loss for the year from these products.

	SW38 (£)	TX39 (£)	UY40 (£)	Total (£)
Selling price per unit				
Less: variable costs per unit				
Direct material				
Direct labour				
Contribution per unit				
Sales volume (units)				
Total contribution				
Less: fixed costs				44,525
Budgeted ▼				

Drop-down list:

Loss
Profit

Task 7 (16 marks)

Broadsword Ltd has the following budgeted costs per unit for product LN60:

		£
Variable costs	Direct materials	6.25
	Direct labour	4.10
	Overheads	3.65
Total variable costs		14.00
Fixed costs	Overheads	12.00
Total costs		26.00

Product LN60 has a selling price of £39 per unit. Budgeted sales volume is 5000 units.

(a) **Calculate the budgeted fixed overheads for LN60.**

The budgeted fixed overheads for product LN60 are: £ [   ].

(b) **Calculate the breakeven volume in units for LN60.**

The breakeven volume for LN60 is [   ] units.

(c) **Using your answer from part (b), calculate the margin of safety in units and the margin of safety (%) if Broadsword sells 4000 units of LN60.**

	Forecast 4000 units
Margin of safety in units	
Margin of safety %	

(d) **If Broadsword increases the selling price of LN60 and all the other costs remain the same, what impact will this have on the breakeven point and the margin of safety, assuming no change in sales demand?**

The breakeven point will increase and the margin of safety will decrease. ☐

The breakeven point will stay the same and the margin of safety will increase. ☐

The breakeven point will decrease and the margin of safety will increase. ☐

The breakeven point will stay the same and the margin of safety will decrease. ☐

Broadsword wishes to make a profit of £20,000 on the sale of LN60.

(e) **Complete the table below to calculate the number of units that Broadsword must sell to achieve its target profit of £20,000, the margin of safety (%) and the margin of safety in sales revenue for the target profit assuming that the sales demand, selling price and all costs remain as per the budget.**

	Product LN60
Number of units to be sold to meet target profit	
Revised margin of safety %	
Revised margin of safety in sales revenue	

Task 8 (16 marks)

Broadsword Ltd uses both batch and unit costing, as appropriate, in its plastic moulding department. It is currently costing a new product, RN36B, which will start production in batches of 76,000 units.

It has estimated that the following costs will be incurred in producing one batch of 76,000 units of RN36B:

Product RN36B	£ per batch
Direct materials	2,080
Direct labour	3,810
Variable overheads	2,470
Fixed manufacturing overheads	4,560
Fixed administration, selling and distribution costs	2,280
Total costs	15,200

(a) **Calculate the total cost of one unit of RN36B.**

The total cost of one unit of RN36B is [   ] pence.

(b) **Calculate the full absorption cost of one unit of RN36B.**

The full absorption cost of one unit of RN36B is [   ] pence.

(c) **Calculate the marginal cost of one unit of RN36B.**

The marginal cost of one unit of RN36B is [   ] pence.

(d) **Calculate the marginal production cost of one batch of RN36B.**

The marginal production cost of one batch of RN36B is £ [   ].

(e) **Calculate the full absorption cost of one batch of RN36B.**

The full absorption cost of one batch of RN36B is £ [   ].

....

Task 9 (16 marks)

Broadsword Ltd budgeted to manufacture 15,000 batches of product WC88 last month. The budgeted and actual costs for the month were as follows:

	Budget	Actual
Number of batches	15,000	17,250
		£
Raw material PG6	32,500	40,065
Raw material EM52	26,800	28,625
Skilled labour	36,800	40,260
Unskilled labour	27,400	34,870
Variable overheads	48,400	49,630
Fixed overheads	58,750	69,280

All operating costs are variable except the fixed overheads.

Complete the table below to show a flexed budget and the resulting variances against this budget for the month. Show the actual variance amount for each cost in the column headed 'Variance'. Identify whether the variance is Adverse (Adv) or Favourable (Fav), Do not use brackets or minus signs.

	Flexed budget	Actual	Variance	Adv	Fav
Number of batches		17,250			
	£	£	£		
Raw material PG6		40,065		☐	☐
Raw material EM52		28,625		☐	☐
Skilled labour		40,260		☐	☐
Unskilled labour		34,870		☐	☐
Variable overheads		49,630		☐	☐
Fixed overheads		69,280		☐	☐
Total costs		262,730			

Task 10 (20 marks)

Broadsword Ltd has estimated the net cash flows of a project it is considering undertaking as below. The cost of capital is 15%.

(a) **Complete the table below to calculate the net present value of the project (to the nearest £000). You MUST enter minus signs where appropriate, and round to TWO decimal places.**

	Year 0 £'000	Year 1 £'000	Year 2 £'000	Year 3 £'000
Net cash flows	-753	385	320	185
PV factors	1.0000	0.8696	0.7561	0.6575
Discounted cash flows				
Net present value				

(b) **Based on the net present value calculated in part (a), should Broadsword accept the project?**

Broadsword should accept the project because the net present value is positive. ☐

Broadsword should not accept the project because the net present value is positive. ☐

Broadsword should accept the project because the net present value is negative. ☐

Broadsword should not accept the project because the net present value is negative. ☐

(c) **Complete the table below to show the net cash flows, as per part (a), and the cumulative cash flows for the project, and calculate the payback period in years and months. You MUST enter minus signs where appropriate in order to obtain full marks and enter whole numbers only. Partial months must be rounded up to the next month.**

	Year 0 £'000	Year 1 £'000	Year 2 £'000	Year 3 £'000
Net cash flows				
Cumulative cash flows				

The payback period is [   ] years and [   ] months.

Broadsword requires projects to pay back within 2.5 years.

(d) **Based on the payback period calculated in part (c), should Broadsword accept the project?**

Broadsword should accept the project because the payback period exceeds 2.5 years. ☐

Broadsword should not accept the project because the payback period exceeds 2.5 years. ☐

Broadsword should accept the project because the payback period is less than 2.5 years. ☐

Broadsword should not accept the project because the payback is less than 2.5 years. ☐

(e) **What is the internal rate of return (IRR) of a project?**

The return the company could have made by investing the money elsewhere ☐

The discount factor that results in a positive net present value ☐

The discount factor that results in a negative net present value ☐

The discount factor that results in a net present value of zero ☐

(f) **What is the approximate internal rate of return (IRR) of the project in part (a)?**

0% ☐

10% ☐

15% ☐

20% ☐

AAT AQ2013 SAMPLE ASSESSMENT 1
COSTS AND REVENUES

ANSWERS

Task 1 (16 marks)

(a)

Material PS99	Receipts			Issues			Balance	
Date	Quantity (kg)	Cost per kg (£)	Total cost (£)	Quantity (kg)	Cost per kg (£)	Total cost (£)	Quantity (kg)	Total cost (£)
Balance at 1 December							8,000	18,000
6 December	4,800	2.150	10,320				12,800	28,320
13 December				7,200	2.250	16,200	5,600	12,120
20 December	12,000	2.210	26,520				17,600	38,640
27 December				4,800	2.167	10,400	12,800	28,240

(b)   Using the LIFO method, the issue of 7,200 kilograms to production on 13 December would be valued at a total of £ | 15,720 |.

....

Task 2 (16 marks)

Date	Code		Dr (£)	Cr (£)
10 December	6400 Plastic extrusion direct costs	▼	5,300	
10 December	5000 Wages control account	▼		5,300
12 December	6500 Plastic moulding direct costs	▼	6,600	
12 December	5000 Wages control account	▼		6,600
14 December	7200 Operating overheads	▼	1,400	
14 December	5000 Wages control account	▼		1,400
16 December	8300 Non-operating overheads	▼	2,600	
16 December	5000 Wages control account	▼		2,600

....

Task 3 (12 marks)

(a)

Pay rate	Hours	£
Basic pay (including basic hours for overtime	484	5,808
Overtime premium rate 1	74	222
Overtime premium rate 2	92	552
Total cost before team bonus	650	6,582
Bonus payment		7,200
Total cost including team bonus		13,782

(b)   The direct labour cost per equivalent unit for December is £ 0.5992 .

(c)   The equivalent units of production with regard to labour for January will be 24,000 and the bonus payable will be £ 10,000 .

Task 4 (18 marks)

	Basis of apportionment	Plastic extrusion £	Plastic moulding £	Maintenance £	Stores £	General administration £	Totals £
Depreciation charge for machinery	Carrying amount of machinery ▼	83,330	44,870				128,200
Variable machine running costs	Number of machine hrs ▼	65,348	30,752				96,100
Rent and rates of premises	Floor space ▼	7,290	7,290	2,430	4,860	2,430	24,300
Light, heat and power for premises	Floor space ▼	4,830	4,830	1,610	3,220	1,610	16,100
Indirect labour	Allocated ▼			15,200	18,240	20,900	54,340
Totals		160,798	87,742	19,240	26,320	24,940	319,040
Reapportion Maintenance		13,468	5,772	19,240			
Reapportion Stores		17,108	9,212		26,320		
Reapportion General administration		12,470	12,470			24940	
Total overheads to profit centres		203,844	115,196				319,040

Task 5 (15 marks)

(a)

Quarter 1 budget	Plastic moulding £		Plastic extrusion £	
Budgeted overhead absorption rate	72.30	per hour	68.10	per hour

(b)

Quarter 1 budget	Plastic moulding £		Plastic extrusion £	
Budgeted overhead absorption rate	22.50	per hour	24.80	per hour

(c) In Quarter 1 overheads for the plastic moulding department were Over-absorbed ▼ by £ 10,000 .

Task 6 (20 marks)

	SW38 (£)	TX39 (£)	UY40 (£)	Total (£)
Selling price per unit	6.50	7.20	8.10	
Less: variable costs per unit				
Direct material	2.10	2.40	2.70	
Direct labour	1.80	2.20	2.50	
Contribution per unit	2.60	2.60	2.90	
Sales volume (units)	15,000	18,000	20,250	
Total contribution	39,000	46,800	58,725	144,525
Less: fixed costs				44,525
Budgeted profit ▼				100,000

Task 7 (16 marks)

(a) The budgeted fixed overhead for product LN60 are: £ | 60,000 |.

(b) The breakeven volume for LN60 is | 2,400 | units.

(c)

	Forecast 4000 units
Margin of safety in units	1,600
Margin of safety %	40

(d) The breakeven point will increase and the margin of safety will decrease. ☐

The breakeven point will stay the same and the margin of safety will increase. ☐

The breakeven point will decrease and the margin of safety will increase. ☑

The breakeven point will stay the same and the margin of safety will decrease. ☐

(e)

	Product LN60
Number of units to be sold to meet target profit	3,200
Revised margin of safety %	36
Revised margin of safety in sales revenue	70,200

Task 8 (16 marks)

(a) The total cost of one unit of RN36B is | 20 | pence.

(b) The full absorption cost of one unit of RN36B is | 17 | pence.

(c) The marginal cost of one unit of RN36B is | 11 | pence.

(d) The marginal production cost of one batch of RN36B is £ | 8,360 |.

(e) The full absorption cost of one batch of RN36B is £ | 12,920 |.

Task 9 (16 marks)

	Flexed budget	Actual	Variance	Adv	Fav
Number of batches	17,250	17,250			
	£	£	£		
Raw material PG6	37,375	40,065	2,690	√	☐
Raw material EM52	30,820	28,625	2,195	☐	√
Skilled labour	42,320	40,260	2,060	☐	√
Unskilled labour	31,510	34,870	3,360	√	☐
Variable overheads	55,660	49,630	6,030	☐	√
Fixed overheads	58,750	69,280	10,530	√	☐
Total costs	256,435	262,730	6,295		

Task 10 (20 marks)

(a)

	Year 0 £'000	Year 1 £'000	Year 2 £'000	Year 3 £'000
Net cash flows	-753	385	320	185
PV factors	1.000	0.8696	0.7561	0.6575
Discounted cash flows	-753.00	334.80	241.95	121.64
Net present value	-54.61			

(b)

Broadsword should accept the project because the net present value is positive.	☐
Broadsword should not accept the project because the net present value is positive.	☐
Broadsword should accept the project because the net present value is negative.	☐
Broadsword should not accept the project because the net present value is negative.	√

(c)

	Year 0 £'000	Year 1 £'000	Year 2 £'000	Year 3 £'000
Net cash flows	-753	385	320	185
Cumulative cash flows	-753	-368	-48	137

The payback period is [2] years and [4] months.

(d)

Broadsword should accept the project because the payback period exceeds 2.5 years. ☐

Broadsword should not accept the project because the payback period exceeds 2.5 years. ☐

Broadsword should accept the project because the payback period is less than 2.5 years. ☑

Broadsword should not accept the project because the payback is less than 2.5 years. ☐

(e)

The return the company could have made by investing the money elsewhere ☐

The discount factor that results in a positive net present value ☐

The discount factor that results in a negative net present value ☐

The discount factor that results in a net present value of zero ☑

(f)

0% ☐

10% ☑

15% ☐

20% ☐

AAT AQ2013 SAMPLE ASSESSMENT 2
COSTS AND REVENUES

Time allowed: 2½ hours

Task 1.1 (16 marks)

Central Bus Company Ltd uses lubricant OR18 in servicing its buses. The inventory record for OR18 for the second half of December has only been partially completed.

Issues of OR18 are made using the first in first out basis (FIFO).

(a) **Complete all the remaining entries in December's inventory record for the receipts and issues of OR18. Cost per litre entries should be completed in £s to two decimal places. Note: Only one entry is permitted per inventory record cell.**

Inventory record – OR18

Date	Receipts			Issues			Balance	
	Quantity litres	Cost per litre (£)	Total cost (£)	Quantity litres	Cost per litre (£)	Total cost (£)	Quantity litres	Total cost (£)
Balance 15 December							4,000	3,360
18 December	5,000		4,400					
24 December				3,000				
30 December		0.92	1,840					
31 December				4,000				

Below is an extract from the inventory control policy for OR18:

'OR18 should be ordered in quantities of 5,000 litres when the inventory balance falls below 5,000 litres.'

(b) **Complete the following sentences.**

The policy of ordering OR18 in quantities of 5,000 litres has been complied with...

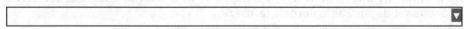

Drop-down list:

for the receipt on 18 December but not for the receipt on 30 December.
for the receipt on 30 December but not for the receipt on 18 December.
for the receipt on 18 December and for the receipt on 30 December.
for neither the receipt on 18 December nor the receipt on 30 December.

The policy of reordering OR18 when the inventory balance falls below 5,000 litres has been complied with...

▼

Drop-down list:

for the receipts on 18 December and 30 December.
for the receipt on 18 December but not for the receipt on 30 December.
for the receipt on 30 December but not for the receipt on 18 December.
for neither the receipt on 18 December nor the receipt on 30 December.

Task 1.2 (16 marks)

A number of transactions took place during December that need to be entered into the cost accounting records of Central Bus Company Ltd.

The following cost accounting codes are used:

Code	Description
2100	Motor oil MO64
2400	Tyres TY13
4000	Bank
4500	Purchase ledger control
5000	Wages control
6100	Contract services direct costs
6200	Scheduled services direct costs
8500	General administration costs

Identify the correct cost accounting entry for each of the following FOUR transactions which took place during December.

(a) **The receipt into inventory of 18 tyres type TY13 at a cost of £152 per tyre. The purchase was made on 28 day credit terms.**

Debit or Credit	Cost Account Code	£
▼		
▼		

Drop-down list:

Credit
Debit

(b) A receipt of 1,500 litres of motor oil MO64 at £1.20 per litre payable immediately by BACS transfer.

Debit or Credit	Cost Account Code	£
▼		
▼		

Drop-down list:

Credit
Debit

(c) Contract services drivers' pay for 480 hours at £11.20 per hour.

Debit or Credit	Cost Account Code	£
▼		
▼		

Drop-down list:

Credit
Debit

(d) Cost of wages for staff in the general administration department who worked 450 hours at £8 per hours.

Debit or Credit	Cost Account Code	£
▼		
▼		

Drop-down list:

Credit
Debit

Task 1.3 (12 marks)

Central Bus Company Ltd's Maintenance department incurred the following times for servicing buses:

	Hours
Normal time hours worked	825
Overtime hours worked (paid at time and a half)	208
Overtime hours worked (paid at double time)	87
Total hours worked	1,120

The maintenance staff's normal time hourly rate at £12 per hour.

Overtime premiums paid are included as part of maintenance labour cost.

Drag and drop the correct entries into the table below to calculate the following FOUR costs:

(a) **The maintenance labour cost of normal time working**
(b) **The maintenance labour cost premium of time and a half working**
(c) **The total maintenance labour cost of double time working**
(d) **The total maintenance labour cost**

	Cost
Calculation (a)	
Calculation (b)	
Calculation (c)	
Calculation (d)	

Empty options:

£1,248	£9,900
£3,744	£13,236
£2,088	£13,440
£1,044	£15,732

Task 1.4 (18 marks)

Central Bus Company (CBC) Ltd has the following information for its two profit centres and three cost centres:

Budgeted overheads	£	£
Diesel fuel and other variable overheads		601,800
Depreciation charge for buses		739,800
Rent and rates of premises		112,400
Light, heat and power at premises		44,000
Departmental specific costs:		
Vehicles Maintenance and Repairs	48,702	
Fuel and Parts Stores	31,500	
General Administration	45,848	
Total departmental specific costs		126,050

Additional information:

Department	Carrying amount of buses (£)	Planned number of miles	Floor space (square metres)
Profit centres:			
Scheduled Services	15,120,000	8,712	
Contract Services	6,480,000	5,808	
Support department cost centres:			
Vehicles Maintenance and Repairs			26,208
Fuel and Parts Stores			15,120
General Administration			9,072
Total	21,600,000	14,520	50,400

Overheads are allocated or apportioned on the most appropriate basis. The total overheads of the three support departments' cost centres are then reapportioned to the bus service profit centres using the direct method.

- 60% of the Vehicles Maintenance and Repairs department's time is spent maintaining the buses in the Scheduled Services profit centre and the remainder in the Contract Services profit centre.

- The Fuel and Parts Stores department makes 65% of its issues to the Scheduled Services profit centre and the remainder to the Contract Services profit centre.

- General Administration support costs can be split 58% to the Scheduled Services profit centre and 42% to the Contract Services profit centre.

- There is no reciprocal servicing between the three support cost centres.

Use the following table to allocate or apportion the overheads using the most appropriate basis. All totals must be entered.

	Basis of apportionment	Scheduled Services £	Contract Services £	Vehicles Maintenance and Repairs £	Fuel and Parts Stores £	General Admini- stration £	Total £
Diesel fuel and other variable overheads	▼						
Depreciation charge for buses	▼						
Departmental specific costs	▼						
Rent and rates at premises	▼						
Light, head and power at premises	▼						
Totals							
Reapportion Vehicles Maintenance and Repairs							
Reapportion Fuel and Parts stores							
Reapportion General Administration							
Total overheads to profit centres							

Drop-down list:

Allocated
Carrying amount of buses
Floor space
Planned number of miles

Task 1.5 (15 marks)

Central Bus Company Ltd. has the following information about one of its routes:

Costs and overheads	£
Fuel and other direct costs per mile	3.20
Drivers' costs per mile	2.80
Total variable operating overheads	16,000
Total fixed operating overheads	24,000
Administration costs	12,000
Other information	
Number of miles in route	8,000

(a) **Calculate the following costs per mile:**

   (i) **Prime cost.**

   The prime cost per mile is: £ [   ] .

   (ii) **Marginal cost per mile. Give your answer to two decimal places.**

   The marginal cost per mile is: £ [   ] .

   (iii) **Full absorption cost per mile. Give your answer to two decimal places.**

   The full absorption cost per mile is: £ [   ] .

(b) **Which of the following costing principles gives the lowest reported profit?**

Prime cost	☐
Marginal cost	☐
Full absorption cost	☐

(c) **Which of the following costing principles gives the highest reported profit?**

Prime cost	☐
Marginal cost	☐
Full absorption cost	☐

Task 1.6 (20 marks)

Central Bus Company Ltd is negotiating a new contract with a customer that is expected to be for 14,000 miles annually. It is possible, however, that this could increase to either 15,600 or 18,200 miles.

Budgeted revenues, costs and profit are shown for 14,000 annual miles in the table to the right. Fixed costs remain fixed across the range being considered.

Budgeted profit statement	£
Sales revenue	182,000
Variable costs:	
– Diesel fuel	16,800
– Drivers' wages and related costs	11,200
– Overheads	15,400
Fixed costs:	
– Indirect labour	19,600
– Overheads	35,000
Total cost	98,000
Total profit	84,000
Profit per mile	6.00

Answer each of the following questions.

Question	Answer
What is the sales revenue per mile if the contract is for 14,000 miles?	
What is the variable cost per mile if the contract is for 18,200 miles?	
What is the fixed cost per mile if the contract is for 15,600 miles?	
What is the total cost per mile if the contract is for 15,600 miles?	
What is the profit per mile if the contract is for 18,200 miles?	

Task 1.7 (16 marks)

Central Bus Company (CBC) Ltd's Contract Services department has prepared the following forecasts for two new routes, CS21 and CS22, which it will be running in Quarter 1 next year.

Forecasts for Quarter 1	CS21	CS22
Sales revenue per mile	£17.00	£18.00
Contribution per mile	£8.00	£10.00
Quarter 1 fixed costs	£16,000	£14,500

(a) **On the basis of the forecasts for Quarter 1, calculate the following ANNUAL figures.**

The forecast break even mileage for CS21 is: [   ] miles.

The forecast break even revenue figure for CS22 is: £ [   ].

A revised forecast has now been produced. There is no change to either contribution per mile, but due to an improved forecast the break even points and budgeted miles have both been revised.

Revised forecasts	CS21	CS22
Sales revenue per mile (unchanged)	£17.00	£18.00
Contribution per mile (unchanged)	£8.00	£10.00
Breakeven point (miles)	9,000	6,000
Forecast miles for route	9,800	7,200

(b) **Calculate the following figures based on the revised information given.**

CS21 margin of safety is: [   ] miles.

CS22 margin of safety in revenue is: £ [   ].

(c) **Based on the revised forecast, calculate the margin of safety for CS21 as a percentage to TWO decimal places.**

CS21 margin of safety: [   ] %

CBC has a target profit for CS21 of £6,000 per quarter, and for CS22 of £7,000 per quarter. Fixed costs remain unchanged from part (a). The company wishes to know what the ANNUAL mileage and sales will have to be to reach the target profit.

(d) **Calculate the relevant figures in the table below.**

	CS21	CS22
CS21: Annual mileage required to reach target profit		
CS22: Annual sales required to reach target profit (in £)		£

Task 1.8 (16 marks)

Central Bus Company (CBC) Ltd has produced the following forecasts for next month for three of the routes that it operates – RT19, RT20 and RT21. Each route requires skilled bus drivers.

Under new European Union regulations all bus drivers are required to attend advanced driver training which has been scheduled for next month. This means that there will be a temporary shortage of skilled drivers with only 3,820 driver hours available.

Route	RT19	RT20	RT21	Total
Contribution (£)	43,200	67,200	52,500	162,900
Fixed costs (£)	22,900	35,420	26,000	84,320
Profit from operations (£)	20,300	31,780	26,500	78,580
Miles travelled in route	2,400	4,200	3,750	
Total drivers' time required (hours)	1,200	1,600	1,500	

Complete the table below (to TWO decimal places) to recommend how many miles of routes RT19, RT20 and RT21 CBC should operate during next month to maximise profits.

Note: It is possible to operate only part of the full mileage of any of the three routes.

Route	RT19	RT20	RT21	Total
Contribution per mile (£)				
Contribution per driver hour (£)				
Ranking				
Total driver time available (hours)				
Driver time allocated (hours)				
Number of miles operated				
Total contribution earned (£)				
Less: fixed costs (£)				
Profit/loss made (£)				

Task 1.9 (16 marks)

Central Bus Company (CBC) Ltd had budgeted to operate 40,000 miles on contract route RT35 last quarter. Due to an increase in demand the actual miles operated on this route were 46,000.

All of CBC's operating costs are variable except the fixed overheads.

(a) **Complete the table below to show a flexed budget and the resulting variances against this budget for route RT35 for last quarter. Show the actual variance amount for sales revenue and each cost, in the column headed 'Variance'. Adverse variances must be denoted using either a minus sign or brackets. Enter 0 where any figure is zero.**

	Original budget	Flexed budget	Actual	Variance
Number of miles	40,000	46,000	46,000	
	£	£	£	£
Sales revenue	104,000		125,300	
Less: costs				
Fuel and other variable costs	39,200		48,620	
Drivers' costs	22,000		24,600	
Fixed overheads	22,480		21,950	
Profit from operations	20,320		30,130	

(b) **Referring to your answer for part (a), which one of the variances has had the greatest impact on profit from operations?**

Sales revenue ☐

Fuel and other variable costs ☐

Drivers' costs ☐

Fixed overheads ☐

(c) **Which one of the following might cause an adverse variance for drivers' costs?**

A reduction in the number of drivers' hours ☐

An increase in the hourly rate of pay for drivers ☐

An increase in hours spent maintaining the buses ☐

A reduction in the number of miles travelled ☐

Task 1.10 (20 marks)

Central Bus Company Ltd is considering replacing its IT system. A new system will result in savings in indirect labour and operating costs. At the end of its three-year economic life it will be scrapped.

The following estimates of capital expenditure and cost savings have been produced:

	Year 0 (£'000)	Year 1 (£'000)	Year 2 (£'000)	Year 3 (£'000)
Capital expenditure	220			
Indirect labour cost savings		58	66	72
Operating cost savings		54	76	86

The company's cost of capital is 14%.

(a) **Using the tables below, calculate the net present value (round the discounted cash flows to the nearest £000). You MUST enter minus signs where appropriate in order to obtain full marks.**

	Year 0 (£'000)	Year 1 (£'000)	Year 2 (£'000)	Year 3 (£'000)
Capital expenditure				
Indirect labour cost savings				
Operating cost savings				
Net cash flows				
PV factors	1.0000	0.8772	0.7695	0.6750
Discounted cash flows				
Net present value				

(b) **Calculate the payback period (round up to the nearest whole month).**

You MUST enter minus signs where appropriate in order to obtain full marks.

	Year 0 (£'000)	Year 1 (£'000)	Year 2 (£'000)	Year 3 (£'000)
Net cash flows				
Cumulative net cash flows				

The payback period is [   ] years and [   ] months.

AAT AQ2013 SAMPLE ASSESSMENT 2
COSTS AND REVENUES

ANSWERS

Task 1.1 (16 marks)

Inventory record – OR18

Date	Receipts						Balance	
	Quantity litres	Cost per litre (£)	Total cost (£)	Quantity litres	Cost per litre (£)	Total cost (£)	Quantity litres	Total cost (£)
Balance 15 December							4,000	3,360
18 December	5,000	0.88	4,400				9,000	7,760
24 December				3,000	0.84	2,520	6,000	5,240
30 December	2,000	0.92	1,840				8,000	7,080
31 December				4,000	0.87**	3,480*	4,000	3,600

*Using FIFO, there are 1,000 units left from the 15 December balance valued at £0.84 per litre. We then need to use 3,000 units from the 18 December receipt at £0.88 per litre.

$(1,000 \times £0.84) + (3,000 \times £0.88) = £3,480$

** £3,840 / 4,000 = £0.87 per litre

Below is an extract from the inventory control policy for OR18:

'OR18 should be ordered in quantities of 5,000 litres when the inventory balance falls below 5,000 litres'.

(b) Complete the following sentences.

The policy of ordering OR18 in quantities of 5,000 litres has been complied with...

for the receipt on 18 December but not for the receipt on 30 December.	

The policy of reordering OR18 when the inventory balance falls below 5,000 litres has been complied with...

for the receipt on 18 December but not for the receipt on 30 December.	

Task 1.2 (16 marks)

(a) The receipt into inventory of 18 tyres type TY13 at a cost of £152 per tyre. The purchase was made on 28 day credit terms.

Debit or Credit	Cost Account Code	£
Debit ▼	2,400	(18 × 152 =) 2,736
Credit ▼	4,500	2,736

(b) A receipt of 1,500 litres of motor oil MO64 at £1.20 per litre payable immediately by BACS transfer.

Debit or Credit	Cost Account Code	£
Debit ▼	2,100	(1,500 × 1.20 =) 1,800
Credit ▼	4,000	1,800

(c) Contract services drivers' pay for 480 hours at £11.20 per hour.

Debit or Credit	Cost Account Code	£
Debit ▼	6,100	(480 × 11.20 =) 5,376
Credit ▼	5,000	5,376

(d) Cost of wages for staff in the general administration department who worked 450 hours at £8 per hours.

Debit or Credit	Cost Account Code	£
Debit ▼	8,500	(450 × 8 =) 3,600
Credit ▼	5,000	3,600

Task 1.3 (12 marks)

Drag and drop the correct entries into the table below to calculate the following FOUR costs:

(a) The maintenance labour cost of normal time working
(b) The maintenance labour cost premium of time and a half working
(c) The total maintenance labour cost of double time working
(d) The total maintenance labour cost

	Cost
Calculation (a)	£9,900
Calculation (b)	£1,248
Calculation (c)	£2,088
Calculation (d)	£15,732

Empty options:

£3,744	£13,236

	£13,440

£1,044

Workings

(a) Normal working time = 825 hours × £12 = £9,900

(b) Premium cost of time and a half = 208 hours × £6 = £1,248 (Remember that the premium is just the extra amount which is paid per hour on top of the normal £12 per hour.)

(c) Total cost of double time working = 87 hours × (£12 + £12) = £2,088

(d) Total labour cost   = Hours at basic rate + hours at £6 premium + hours at £12 premium

= [(825 + 208 + 87) × £12] + (208 × £6) + (87 × £12)

= £13,440 + £1,248 + £1,044

= £15,732

Alternatively you could have calculated (d) as

(825 × £12) + (208 × £18) + (87 × £24) = £15,732

Task 1.4 (18 marks)

Use the following table to allocate or apportion the overheads using the most appropriate basis. All totals must be entered.

	Basis of apportionment	Scheduled Services £	Contract Services £	Vehicles Maintenance and Repairs £	Fuel and Parts Stores £	General Admini- stration £	Total £
Diesel fuel and other variable overheads (W1)	Planned ▼ number of miles	361,080	240,720				601,800
Depreciation charge for buses (W2)	Carrying ▼ amount of buses	517,860	221,940				739,800
Departmental specific costs (W3)	Allocated ▼			48,702	31,500	45,848	126,050
Rent and rates at premises (W4)	Floor space ▼			58,448	33,720	20,232	112,400
Light, head and power at premises (W5)	Floor space ▼			22,880	13,200	7,920	44,000
Totals		878,940	462,660	130,030	78,420	74,000	1,624,050
Reapportion Vehicles Maintenance and Repairs (× 60% and 40%)		78,018	52,012	130,030			
Reapportion Fuel and Parts stores (× 65% and 35%)		50,973	27,447		78,420		
Reapportion General Administration (× 58% and 42%)		42,920	31,080			74,000	
Total overheads to profit centres		1,050,851	573,199				1,624,050

Workings

				$
1	601,800 ×	(8,712 / 14,520)	=	361,080
	601,800 ×	(5,808 / 14,520)	=	240,720
2	739,800 ×	(15,120 / 21,600)	=	517,860
	739,800 ×	(6,480 / 21,600)	=	221,940
3	Figures taken straight from question			
4	112,400 ×	(26,208 / 50,400)	=	58,448
	112,400 ×	(15,120 / 50,400)	=	33,720
	112,400 ×	(9,072 / 50,400)	=	20,232
5	44,000 ×	(26,208 / 50,400)	=	22,880
	44,000 ×	(15,120 / 50,400)	=	13,200
	44,000 ×	(9,072 / 50,400)	=	7,920

···

Task 1.5 (15 marks)

(a) **Calculate the following costs per mile:**

(i) **Prime cost.**

The prime cost per mile is: £ | 6 | .

(Prime cost means direct cost. Prime cost = £3.20 + £2.80 = £6.00)

(ii) **Marginal cost per mile. Give your answer to two decimal places.**

The marginal cost per mile is: £ | 8 | .

(Marginal cost means variable cost. Marginal cost = £6 + (£16,000 / 8,000) = £8)

(iii) **Full absorption cost per mile. Give your answer to two decimal places.**

The full absorption cost per mile is: £ | 11 | .

(Absorption cost = marginal cost + overhead absorption rate (OAR). OAR = £24,000 / 8,000 = £3 per mile. Absorption cost = £8 + £3 = £11)

(b) **Which of the following costing principles gives the lowest reported profit?**

Prime cost	✓
Marginal cost	☐
Full absorption cost	☐

(c) **Which of the following costing principles gives the highest reported profit?**

Prime cost	☐
Marginal cost	☐
Full absorption cost	☑

Task 1.6 (20 marks)

Answer each of the following questions.

Question	Answer
What is the sales revenue per mile if the contract is for 14,000 miles? (W1)	13
What is the variable cost per mile if the contract is for 18,200 miles? (W2)	3.10
What is the fixed cost per mile if the contract is for 15,600 miles? (W3)	3.50
What is the total cost per mile if the contract is for 15,600 miles? (W4)	6.60
What is the profit per mile if the contract is for 18,200 miles? (W5)	6.90

Workings

1   £182,000 / 14,000 = £13

2   The variable cost per mile for 18,200 miles is the same as the variable cost per mile for 14,000 miles.

     (£16,800 + £11,200 + £15,400) / 14,000 = £3.10

3   (£19,600 + £35,000) / 15,600 = £3.50

4   £3.10 + £3.50 = £6.60

5   Revenue per mile = £13 (from above). Total profit = revenue – variable costs – fixed costs.

     Total profit = (18,200 × £13) – (18,200 × £3.10) - £19,600 – £35,000 = £125,580

     Profit per mile = £125,580 / 18,200 miles = £6.90

Task 1.7 (16 marks)

(a) **On the basis of the forecasts for Quarter 1, calculate the following ANNUAL figures.**

The forecast break even mileage for CS21 is: | 8,000 | miles.

Working

Breakeven point = Fixed costs for the year / Contribution per mile

∴ Breakeven point = (4 × £16,000) / £8 = 8,000 miles

The forecast break even revenue figure for CS22 is: £ | 104,400 | .

Working

Breakeven point = Fixed costs for the year / Contribution per mile

∴ Breakeven point = (4 × £14,500) / £10 = 5,800 miles

Breakeven revenue = breakeven point × revenue per mile

∴ Breakeven revenue = 5,800 miles × £18 = £104,400

A revised forecast has now been produced. There is no change to either contribution per mile, but due to an improved forecast the break even points and budgeted miles have both been revised.

Revised forecasts	CS21	CS22
Sales revenue per mile (unchanged)	£17.00	£18.00
Contribution per mile (unchanged)	£8.00	£10.00
Breakeven point (miles)	9,000	6,000
Forecast miles for route	9,800	7,200

(b) **Calculate the following figures based on the revised information given.**

CS21 margin of safety is: | 800 | miles.

Working

9,800 miles – 9,000 miles = 800 miles

CS22 margin of safety in revenue is: £ | 21,600 | .

7,200 miles – 6,000 miles = 1,200 miles.

1,200 miles × £18 = £21,600

(c) **Based on the revised forecast, calculate the margin of safety for CS21 as a percentage to TWO decimal places.**

CS21 margin of safety: | 8.16 | %

(800 / 9,800) × 100% = 8.16%

CBC has a target profit for CS21 of £6,000 per quarter, and for CS22 of £7,000 per quarter. Fixed costs remain unchanged from part (a). The company wishes to know what the ANNUAL mileage and sales will have to be to reach the target profit.

(d) **Calculate the relevant figures in the table below.**

	CS21	CS22
CS21: Annual mileage required to reach target profit (W1)	11,000	
CS22: Annual sales required to reach target profit (in £) (W2)		£ 154,800

Workings

1   Mileage to reach target profit = (Fixed costs + target profit) / Contribution per mile

∴ Mileage to reach target profit = (£64,000 + £24,000) / £8 = 11,000 miles

2   Mileage to reach target profit = (£58,000 + £28,000) / £10 = 8,600 miles

∴ Revenue to reach target profit = 8,600 miles × £18 = £154,800

Task 1.8 (16 marks)

Complete the table below (to TWO decimal places) to recommend how many miles of routes RT19, RT20 and RT21 CBC should operate during next month to maximise profits.

Note: It is possible to operate only part of the full mileage of any of the three routes.

Route	RT19	RT20	RT21	Total
Contribution per mile (£) (Contribution ÷ miles travelled)	18	16	14	
Contribution per driver hour (£) (Contribution ÷ drivers' time)	36	42	35	
Ranking	2	1	3	
Total driver time available (hours)				3,820
Driver time allocated (hours)	1,200	1,600	1,020	
Number of miles operated	2,400	4,200	2,550*	
Total contribution earned (£) (Contribution per mile × miles operated)	43,200	67,200	35,700	146,100
Less: fixed costs (£)				84,320
Profit/loss made (£)				61,780

* (1,020 / 1,500) × 3,750 = 2,550

Task 1.9 (16 marks)

(a) **Complete the table below to show a flexed budget and the resulting variances against this budget for route RT35 for last quarter. Show the actual variance amount for sales revenue and each cost, in the column headed 'Variance'. Adverse variances must be denoted using either a minus sign or brackets. Enter 0 where any figure is zero.**

	Original budget	Flexed budget	Actual	Variance
Number of miles	40,000	46,000	46,000	
	£	£	£	£
Sales revenue (W1)	104,000	119,600	125,300	5,700
Less: costs				
Fuel and other variable costs (W2)	39,200	45,080	48,620	-3,540
Drivers' costs (W3)	22,000	25,300	24,600	700
Fixed overheads (W4)	22,480	22,480	21,950	530
Profit from operations	20,320	26,740	30,130	

Workings

1   (104,000 / 40,000) × 46,000 = £119,600

2   (39,200 / 40,000) × 46,000 = £45,080

3   (22,000 / 40,000) × 46,000 = £25,300

4   Fixed overheads do not change with the number of miles

(b) **Referring to your answer for part (a), which one of the variances has had the greatest impact on profit from operations?**

Sales revenue	✓
Fuel and other variable costs	☐
Drivers' costs	☐
Fixed overheads	☐

(c) **Which one of the following might cause an adverse variance for drivers' costs?**

A reduction in the number of drivers' hours	☐
An increase in the hourly rate of pay for drivers	☑
An increase in hours spent maintaining the buses	☐
A reduction in the number of miles travelled	☐

Task 1.10 (20 marks)

(a) **Using the tables below, calculate the net present value (round the discounted cash flows to the nearest £'000). You MUST enter minus signs where appropriate in order to obtain full marks.**

	Year 0 £'000	Year 1 £'000	Year 2 £'000	Year 3 £'000
Capital expenditure	−220			
Indirect labour cost savings		58	66	72
Operating cost savings		54	76	86
Net cash flows	−220	112	142	158
PV factors	1.0000	0.8772	0.7695	0.6750
Discounted cash flows	−220	98	109	107
Net present value	94			

(b) **Calculate the payback period (round up to the nearest whole month).**

You MUST enter minus signs where appropriate in order to obtain full marks.

	Year 0 £'000	Year 1 £'000	Year 2 £'000	Year 3 £'000
Net cash flows	−220	112	142	158
Cumulative net cash flows	−220	−108	34	192

The payback period is ☐ 1 ☐ years and ☐ 10 ☐ months.

BPP PRACTICE ASSESSMENT 1
COSTS AND REVENUES

Time allowed: 2½ hours

Costs and Revenues BPP practice assessment 1

Task 1

The inventory record shown below for plastic grade FIBREGLASS PANELS for the month of July has only been fully completed for the first three weeks of the month. The EOQ for fibreglass panels is 791 kg.

(a) **Complete ALL entries in the inventory record for the month and for the closing balance at the end of July, using the AVCO method of issuing inventory.**

(Show the costs per kilogram (kg) in £s to 3 decimal places and the total costs in whole £s).

Inventory record for plastic grade FIBREGLASS PANELS

Date	Receipts Quantity kg	Receipts Cost per kg (£)	Receipts Total cost (£)	Issues Quantity kg	Issues Cost per kg (£)	Issues Total cost (£)	Balance Quantity kg	Balance Total cost (£)
Balance as at 22 July							120	276
24 July		2.320						
26 July				300				
28 July		2.350						
31 July				400				

(b) **Complete the sentence below.**

Using the FIFO method, the issue of 300 kg to production on 26 July would have been valued at a total of

£ [   ]

....

Task 2

Drag and drop the correct entries into the Journal below to record the following FOUR accounting transactions:

1. Receipt of metal widgets into inventory paying by BACS.
2. Issue of metal widgets from inventory to production.
3. Receipt of metal widgets into inventory paying on credit.
4. Return of metal widgets from production to inventory.

The drag and drop choices are:

- Dr. Inventory, Cr. Trade Payables' Control
- Dr. Inventory, Cr. Production
- Dr. Inventory, Cr. Bank
- Dr. Bank, Cr. Goods inward
- Dr. Trade Payables' Control, Cr. Goods inward
- Dr. Production, Cr. Inventory

	Drag and drop choice
Transaction 1	
Transaction 2	
Transaction 3	
Transaction 4	

Task 3

Below is a table showing the hours worked by one of Savoyard Ltd's employees, who is paid as follows:

- For a basic shift every day from Monday to Friday, the basic pay is £25 per hour.

- For any overtime in excess of the basic hours, on any day from Monday to Friday – the extra hours are paid at time-and-a-half (basic pay plus an overtime premium equal to half of basic pay).

- For any hours worked on Saturday or Sunday the hours are paid at double time (basic pay plus an overtime premium equal to basic pay).

(a) **Complete the gaps in the table below to calculate the labour cost.**

Employee's weekly timesheet for week ending 7 July

	Hours	Total pay £
Basic pay (including basic hours for overtime)	52	
Mon-Fri overtime premium	2	
Sat-Sun overtime premium	6	
Total	**60**	

(b) Employees are also entitled to a bonus of 30% of basic hourly rate for every unit of production in excess of the monthly target. The target for last month was 500 units and employee A produced 526 units.

What was employee A's bonus payment for the month?

£

(c) At the end of the month there was a total closing work-in-progress of 5,000 units which were 75% complete with regard to labour.

What are the equivalent units of production with regard to labour of the closing work-in-progress?

units

Task 4

Claridges Ltd's budgeted overheads for the next financial year are:

	£	£
Depreciation of plant and equipment		2,010,375
Power for production machinery		1,787,500
Rent and rates		261,250
Light and heat		57,750
Indirect labour costs:		
Maintenance	252,875	
Stores	90,125	
General Administration	600,250	
Total indirect labour cost		943,250

The following information is also available:

Department	Net book value of plant and equipment	Production machinery power usage (KwH)	Floor space (square metres)	Number of employees
Production centres:				
Metal bashing	14,000,000	5,362,500		15
Metal extrusion	6,000,000	3,575,000		10
Support cost centres:				
Maintenance			35,000	5
Stores			21,000	2
General Administration			14,000	7
Total	20,000,000	8,937,500	70,000	39

Overheads are allocated or apportioned on the most appropriate basis. The total overheads of the support cost centres are then reapportioned to the two production centres using the direct method.

- 76% of the Maintenance cost centre's time is spent maintaining production machinery in the Metal bashing production centre, and the remainder in the Metal extrusion production centre.

- The Stores cost centre makes 60% of its issues to the Metal bashing production centre, and 40% to the Metal extrusion production centre.

- General Administration supports the two production centres equally.

- There is no reciprocal servicing between the three support cost centres.

Complete the table, showing the apportionment and reapportionment of overheads to the two production centres:

	Basis of apportionment	Metal bashing £	Metal extrusion £	Maintenance £	Stores £	General Admin £	Totals £
Depreciation of plant and equipment	NBV of plant and equipment						
Power for production machinery	Production machinery power usage (KwH)						
Rent and rates	Floor space						
Light and heat	Floor space						
Indirect labour	Allocated						
Totals							
Reapportion Maintenance							
Reapportion Stores							
Reapportion General Admin							
Total overheads to production centres							

Task 5

Next quarter Claridges Ltd's budgeted overheads and activity levels are:

	Metal bashing	Metal extrusion
Budgeted overheads (£)	814,990	445,500
Budgeted direct labour hours	40,750	24,750
Budgeted machine hours	13,145	8,250

(a) **What would be the budgeted overhead absorption rate for each department, if this were set based on their both being heavily automated?**

☐ Metal bashing £20/hour, Metal extrusion £18/hour

☐ Metal bashing £20/hour, Metal extrusion £54/hour

☐ Metal bashing £62/hour, Metal extrusion £18/hour

☐ Metal bashing £62/hour, Metal extrusion £54/hour

(b) **What would be the budgeted overhead absorption rate for each department, if this were set based on their both being labour intensive?**

☐ Metal bashing £20/hour, Metal extrusion £18/hour

☐ Metal bashing £20/hour, Metal extrusion £54/hour

☐ Metal bashing £62/hour, Metal extrusion £18/hour

☐ Metal bashing £62/hour, Metal extrusion £54/hour

Additional data

At the end of the quarter actual overheads incurred were found to be:

	Metal bashing	Metal extrusion
Actual overheads (£)	789,765	495,250

(c) **Assuming that exactly the same amount of overheads was absorbed as budgeted, what were the budgeted under- or over-absorptions in the quarter?**

☐ Metal bashing over-absorbed £25,225, Metal extrusion over-absorbed £49,750

☐ Metal bashing over-absorbed £25,225, Metal extrusion under-absorbed £49,750

☐ Metal bashing under-absorbed £25,225, Metal extrusion under-absorbed £49,750

☐ Metal bashing under-absorbed £25,225, Metal extrusion over-absorbed £49,750

Task 6

Claridges Ltd has prepared a forecast for the next quarter for one of its small Metal components, the zigger. This component is produced in batches and the forecast is based on selling and producing 3,000 batches.

One of the customers of Claridges Ltd has indicated that it may be significantly increasing its order level for the zigger for the next quarter, and it appears that activity levels of 5,000 batches and 7,000 batches are feasible.

The semi-variable costs should be calculated using the high-low method. If 7,500 batches are sold the total semi-variable cost will be £18,450, and there is a constant unit variable cost up to this volume.

Complete the table below and calculate the estimated profit per batch of the zigger at the different activity levels:

Batches produced and sold	3,000	5,000	7,000
	£	£	£
Sales revenue	90,000		
Variable costs:			
• Direct materials	13,500		
• Direct labour	31,500		
• Overheads	18,000		
Semi-variable costs:	9,450		
• Variable element			
• Fixed element			
Total cost	72,450		
Total profit	17,550		
Profit per batch (to 2 decimal places)	5.85		

Task 7

Claridges Ltd manufactures the alphapop, which has a selling price of £20 per unit, and a total variable cost of £12 per unit. Claridges Ltd estimates that the fixed costs per quarter associated with this product are £46,000.

(a) **Calculate the budgeted breakeven, in units, for the alphapop.**

	units

(b) **Calculate the budgeted breakeven, in £s, for the alphapop.**

£	

(c) **Complete the table below to show the budgeted margin of safety in units and the margin of safety percentage if Claridges Ltd sells 6,000 units or 7,000 units of the alphapop:**

Units of alphapop sold	6,000	7,000
	£	£
Margin of safety (units)		
Margin of safety percentage		

(d) **If Claridges Ltd wishes to make a profit of £20,000, how many units of the alphapop must it sell?**

	units

(e) **If Claridges Ltd increases the selling price of the alphapop by £5 what will be the impact on the breakeven point and the margin of safety, assuming no change in the number of units sold?**

☐ The breakeven point will decrease and the margin of safety will increase.

☐ The breakeven point will stay the same but the margin of safety will decrease.

☐ The breakeven point will decrease and the margin of safety will stay the same.

☐ The breakeven point will increase and the margin of safety will decrease.

Task 8

The Metal extrusion department of Claridges Ltd uses batch costing for some of its products.

The product DD1 is made in one batch of 62,000 units and the budgeted costs are as follows.

Description	Cost per batch £
Direct material	77,500
Direct labour	83,700
Variable overheads	12,400
Fixed manufacturing overheads	31,000
Fixed administration, selling and distribution costs	18,600
Total costs	223,200

(a) **Calculate the total cost of one unit of DD1.**

The total cost of one unit of DD1 is £ _____

(b) **Calculate the full absorption cost of one unit of DD1**

The full absorption cost of one unit of DD1 is £ _____

(c) **Calculate the marginal cost of one unit of DD1**

The marginal cost of one unit of DD1 is £ _____

(d) **Calculate the marginal production cost of one batch of DD1**

The marginal production cost of one batch of DD1 is £ _____

(e) **Calculate the full absorption cost of one batch of DD1.**

The full absorption cost of one batch of DD1 is £ _____

Task 9

Claridges Ltd has the following original budget and actual performance for the BEPPO for the year ending 31 July:

	Budget	Actual
Volume sold	250,000	360,000
	£'000	£'000
Sales revenue	5,000	9,000
Less costs:		
Direct materials	875	1,325
Direct labour	1,000	1,200
Overheads	2,450	3,070
Operating profit	675	3,405

Both direct materials and direct labour are variable costs, but the overheads are fixed.

Complete the table below to show a flexed budget and the resulting variances against this budget for the year. Show the actual variance amount for sales, each cost, and operating profit, in the column headed 'Variance' and indicate whether this is Favourable or Adverse by entering F or A in the final column. If neither F nor A enter 0.

	Flexed Budget	Actual	Variance	Favourable F or Adverse A
Volume sold		360,000		
	£'000	£'000	£'000	
Sales revenue		9,000		
Less costs:				
Direct materials		1,325		
Direct labour		1,200		
Overheads		3,070		
Operating profit		3,405		

Task 10

One of the extrusion machines in the Metal extrusion department is nearing the end of its useful life and Claridges Ltd is considering purchasing a replacement machine.

Estimates have been made for the initial capital cost, sales income and operating costs of the replacement machine, which is expected to have a useful life of three years:

	Year 0 £'000	Year 1 £'000	Year 2 £'000	Year 3 £'000
Capital expenditure	2,250			
Other cash flows:				
Sales income		1,050	1,400	2,000
Operating costs		300	375	475

The company appraises capital investment projects using a 15% cost of capital.

(a) **Complete the table below and calculate the net present value of the proposed replacement machine (to the nearest £'000):**

	Year 0 £'000	Year 1 £'000	Year 2 £'000	Year 3 £'000
Capital expenditure				
Sales income				
Operating costs				
Net cash flows				
PV factors	1.0000	0.8696	0.7561	0.6575
Discounted cash flows				
Net present value				

The net present value is [＿＿＿＿＿] ▾.

Picklist:

Positive
Negative

(b) **Calculate the payback period of the proposed replacement machine to the nearest whole month.**

The payback period is [＿＿＿＿＿] year(s) and [＿＿＿＿＿] month(s).

(c) The net present value of an investment at 12% is £24,000 and at 20% the net present value is -£8,000.

What is the internal rate of return of the investment?

☐ 6%

☐ 12%

☐ 18%

☐ 20%

BPP PRACTICE ASSESSMENT 1
COSTS AND REVENUES

ANSWERS

Costs and Revenues BPP practice assessment 1

Task 1

(a) Inventory record card

Date	Receipts Quantity kg	Cost per kg (£)	Total cost (£)	Issues Quantity kg	Cost per kg (£)	Total cost (£)	Balance Quantity kg	Total cost (£)
Balance as at 22 July							120	276
24 July	791	2.320	1,835				911	2,111
26 July				300	2.317	695	611	1,416
28 July	791	2.350	1,859				1,402	3,275
31 July				400	2.336	934	1,002	2,341

(b)

£693.60

120 units	£276.00
180 units @ £2.320	£417.60
300 units	£693.60

Task 2

	Drag and drop choice
Transaction 1	Dr. Inventory, Cr. Bank
Transaction 2	Dr. Production, Cr. Inventory
Transaction 3	Dr. Inventory, Cr. Trade payables' Control
Transaction 4	Dr. Inventory, Cr. Production

Task 3

(a) **Employee's weekly timesheet for week ending 7 July**

	Hours	Total pay £
Basic pay (including basic hours for overtime)	52	1,300
Mon-Fri overtime premium	2	25
Sat – Sun overtime premium	6	150
Total	**60**	1,475

(b) | £195 |

£25 × 30% = £7.50 per unit

26 extra units × £7.50 = £195

(c) | 3,750 | units

5,000 units × 75% = 3,750 units

Task 4

	Basis of apportionment	Metal bashing £	Metal extrusion £	Maintenance £	Stores £	General Admin £	Totals £
Depreciation of plant and equipment	NBV of plant and equipment	1,407,262	603,113				2,010,375
Power for production machinery	Production machinery power usage (KwH)	1,072,500	715,000				1,787,500
Rent and rates	Floor space			130,625	78,375	52,250	261,250
Light and heat	Floor space			28,875	17,325	11,550	57,750
Indirect labour	Allocated			252,875	90,125	600,250	943,250
Totals		2,479,762	1,318,113	412,375	185,825	664,050	5,060,125
Reapportion Maintenance		313,405	98,970	(412,375)			
Reapportion Stores		111,495	74,330		(185,825)		
Reapportion General Admin		332,025	332,025			(664,050)	
Total overheads to production centres		3,236,687	1,823,438				5,060,125

Task 5

(a) The correct answer is Metal bashing £62/hour, Metal extrusion £54/hour

(b) The correct answer is Metal bashing £20/hour, Metal extrusion £18/hour

(c) The correct answer is Metal bashing over-absorbed £25,225, Metal extrusion under-absorbed £49,750

Task 6

Batches produced and sold	3,000	5,000	7,000
	£	£	£
Sales revenue	90,000	150,000	210,000
Variable costs:			
• Direct materials	13,500	22,500	31,500
• Direct labour	31,500	52,500	73,500
• Overheads	18,000	30,000	42,000
Semi-variable costs:	9,450		
• Variable element		10,000	14,000
• Fixed element		3,450	3,450
Total cost	72,450	118,450	164,450
Total profit	17,550	31,550	45,550
Profit per batch (to 2 decimal places)	5.85	6.31	6.51

Task 7

(a) 5,750 units

(b) £115,000

(c)

Units of alphapop sold	6,000	7,000
	£	£
Margin of safety (units)	250	1,250
Margin of safety percentage	4%	18%

(d) 8,250 units

(e) The correct answer is: The breakeven point will decrease and the margin of safety will increase.

Task 8

(a) £3.60

£223,200 / 62,000 = £3.60 per unit

(b) £3.30

$$\frac{223,200 - 18,600}{62,000} = £3.30$$

(c) £2.80

$$\frac{77,500 + 83,700 + 12,400}{62,000} = £2.80$$

(d) £173,600

£2.80 × 62,000 = £173,600

(e) £204,600

£223,200 − 18,600 = £204,600 (or £3.30 × 62,000 = £204,600)

Task 9

	Flexed Budget	Actual	Variance	Favourable F or Adverse A
Volume sold	360,000	360,000		
	£'000	£'000	£'000	
Sales revenue	7,200	9,000	1,800	F
Less costs:				
Direct materials	1,260	1,325	65	A
Direct labour	1,440	1,200	240	F
Overheads	2,450	3,070	620	A
Operating profit	2,050	3,405	1,355	F

Task 10

(a)

	Year 0 £'000	Year 1 £'000	Year 2 £'000	Year 3 £'000
Capital expenditure	(2,250)			
Sales income		1,050	1,400	2,000
Operating costs		(300)	(375)	(475)
Net cash flows	(2,250)	750	1,025	1,525
PV factors	1.0000	0.8696	0.7561	0.6575
Discounted cash flows	(2,250)	652	775	1,003
Net present value	180			

The net present value is **positive.**

(b) The payback period is **2** years and **4** months.

(c) 18%

The IRR is the rate at which the NPV of the project is zero. At 12% the NPV is positive and at 20% the NPV is negative. This means that the IRR must be somewhere in between 12% and 20%. The answer is therefore 18%.

BPP PRACTICE ASSESSMENT 2
COSTS AND REVENUES

Time allowed: 2½ hours

Costs and Revenues BPP practice assessment 2

Task 1

(a) **Choose the correct words from the drop down menu to complete the paragraph.**

If costs are increasing, FIFO/LIFO will give a higher profit than FIFO/LIFO as issues, which form cost of sales, are at the earlier, LOWER/HIGHER prices.

The weighted average method GIVES A HIGHER PROFIT THAN LIFO AND FIFO/GIVES A LOWER PROFIT THAN FIFO AND LIFO/FALLS SOMEWHERE IN BETWEEN THE PROFITS GIVEN BY FIFO AND LIFO.

In the long-term, over the life of the business, any such differences will DISAPPEAR/GIVE THE BUSINESS AN ADVANTAGE/GIVE THE BUSINESS A DISADVANTAGE

(b)

The following data relate to inventory item HMF2.

Average usage   200 units per day

Lead time   16 – 20 days

Reorder level   5,700

What is the approximate number of HMF2 parts carried as buffer inventory?

units

(c) **Which of the following is the correct formula for the economic order quantity?**

☐ $EOQ = \sqrt{\dfrac{2cd}{h}}$

☐ $EOQ = \sqrt{\dfrac{2hd}{c}}$

☐ $EOQ = \dfrac{\sqrt{2hd}}{c}$

☐ $EOQ = \dfrac{\sqrt{2cd}}{h}$

Where   h is the cost of holding one unit in inventory for one year
                 d is the annual demand
                 c is the cost of placing an order

Task 2

The material stores control account for a company for March looks like this:

Material stores control account

	£		£
Balance b/d	30,000	Work in progress	100,000
Suppliers	122,500	Overhead control	30,000
Work in progress	45,000	Balance c/d	67,500
	197,500		197,500
Balance b/d	67,500		

Which of the following statements are correct?

(i)   Issues of direct materials during March were £45,000

(ii) Issues of direct materials during March were £100,000

(iii) Issues of indirect materials during March were £30,000

(iv) Purchases of materials during March were £122,500

☐ (i) and (iv) only

☐ (ii) and (iv) only

☐ (ii), (iii) and (iv) only

☐ All of them

Task 3

(a) **Complete the columns headed Direct wages and Indirect wages.**

(Notes: Zero figures should be entered in cells where appropriate).

		Direct wages £	Indirect wages £
Basic 35 hours per week at £10 per hour			
Overtime of 4 hours due to machine breakdown			
	Basic 4 hrs @ £10		
	Premium 4 hrs @ £5		
Overtime of 2 hrs at the request of customer			
	Basic 2 hrs @ £10		
	Premium 2 hrs @ £5		
Total			

(b) An employee is paid on a differential piecework system on the following basis.

Up to 750 units produced a week	£2.50 per unit
Units over 750 and up to 1,000	£2.88 per unit
Any units over 1,000	£3.35 per unit

In the week ending 29 June the employee produced 1,075 units.

What is his total gross pay for the week?

£ [   ]

Task 4

A manufacturing organisation has two production departments, A and B, and two service cost centres, stores and the canteen.

The budgeted overheads for the next period are as follows:

	Total £	A £	B £	Stores £	Canteen £
Indirect wages	75,700	7,800	4,700	21,200	42,000
Rent	24,000				
Buildings insurance	2,000				
Power	6,400				
Heat and light	4,000				
Supervisor's wages – Dept A	10,000				
Machinery depreciation	3,200				
Machinery insurance	2,200				
Total					
Canteen					(49,730)
Stores					

You are also provided with the following information:

	Total	A	B	Stores	Canteen
Net book value of machinery	£300,000	£140,000	£120,000	£15,000	£25,000
Power usage (%)	100%	45%	30%	5%	20%
Number of employees	126	70	40	10	6
Supervisor's hours	40	25	15		
Floor area (sq m)	30,000	12,000	8,000	4,000	6,000
Materials requisitions	500	300	200		

The stores staff use the canteen but the canteen makes no use of the stores services.

You are required to:

(a) **Allocate or apportion the overheads to each of the production and service cost centres on a fair basis. (Work to the nearest whole £.)**

(b) **Reapportion the service cost centre costs to the production cost centres using the step down method. (Work to the nearest whole £.)**

Task 5

(a) Budgeted machine hours   17,000

    Actual machine hours   21,250

    Budgeted overheads   £85,000

    Actual overheads   £110,500

    Based on the data above:

    The machine hour absorption rate is £ ⬚ per hour.

    The overhead for the period was ⬚▼ absorbed by £ ⬚ .

    Picklist:

    Over-
    Under-

(b) The accounting entries at the end of a period for production overhead under-absorbed would be **(tick the correct boxes)**:

	Debit	Credit	No entry in this a/c
Overhead control account			
Work in progress account			
Statement of profit or loss			

(c) The overhead absorption rate for product M is £8 per machine hour. Each unit of M requires 1 machine hour. Inventories of product M last period were:

	Units
Opening inventory	6,000
Closing inventory	6,750

    The absorption costing profit for the period for product M will be:

    ☐   higher

    ☐   lower

    than the marginal costing profit. The difference between the two profit figures will be

    £ ⬚

Task 6

CCC Ltd has prepared a forecast for the next quarter for one of its products. The products are produced in batches and the forecast is based on selling and producing 4,000 batches.

The managing director would like to expand the business and is interested to know the profits that could be made if 6,000 batches were made and sold and 9,000 batches were made and sold.

The semi-variable costs should be calculated using the high-low method. If 6,500 batches are sold the total semi-variable cost will be £24,250, and there is a constant unit variable cost up to this volume.

Complete the table below and calculate the estimated profit per batch of the product at the different activity levels:

Batches produced and sold	4,000	6,000	9,000
	£	£	£
Sales revenue	140,000		
Variable costs:			
• Direct materials	22,000		
• Direct labour	50,000		
• Overheads	28,000		
Semi-variable costs:	16,750		
Total cost	116,750		
Total profit	23,250		
Profit per batch (to 2 decimal places)	5.81		

Task 7

ABC Co, is a company producing and selling two types of toys: the elephant and the giraffe. The expected monthly costs and sales information for each toy is as follows.

Toy	Elephant	Giraffe
Sales and production quantity	1,250	1,750
Labour hours per month	120	100
Total sales revenue	£2,500	£3,500
Total direct materials	£200	£350
Total direct labour	£750	£875
Total variable overheads	£50	£140

The total expected monthly fixed costs relating to the production of all toys is £750.

(a) **You are required to complete the table below to show the profit volume ratio for each toy.**

Toy	Elephant £	Giraffe £
Selling price per toy		
Less: Unit variable costs		
Direct materials		
Direct labour		
Variable overheads		
Contribution per toy		
Profit volume ratio (%)		

(b) **ABC has decided stop making elephant toys. The expected monthly fixed costs remain at £750. Calculate the breakeven point to the nearest whole unit.**

	units

(c) **Calculate the margin of safety.**

	units

Task 8

(a) JLS Ltd operates a job costing system. The company calculates the cost of the job and then adds 20% profit onto the cost to produce a sales price.

The estimated costs for job EIL are as follows.

Direct materials   3kg @ £5 per kg

Direct labour   4 hours @ £9 per hour

Production overheads are budgeted to be £240,000 for the period and are absorbed on the basis of a total of 30,000 labour hours.

Fill in the table below to calculate the selling price for the job.

Job EIL	£
Direct materials	
Direct labour	
Production overheads	
Total cost	
20% profit	
Selling price for the job	

(b) ABC Ltd uses process costing for some of its products.

Identify the correct journal entries for an abnormal loss:

	Debit	Credit
Process account		
Abnormal loss account		

Task 9

Jumbo Ltd has the following original budget and actual performance for the year ending 31 May:

	Budget	Actual
Volume sold	300,000	410,000
	£'000	£'000
Sales revenue	9,000	14,350
Less costs:		
Direct materials	1,650	2,460
Direct labour	1,350	1,640
Overheads	3,250	4,010
Operating profit	2,750	6,240

Both direct materials and direct labour are variable costs, but the overheads are fixed.

Complete the table below to show a flexed budget and the resulting variances against this budget for the year. Show the actual variance amount for sales, each cost, and operating profit, in the column headed 'Variance' and indicate whether this is Favourable or Adverse by entering F or A in the final column. If the variance is neither F nor A, enter 0.

	Flexed Budget	Actual	Variance	Favourable F or Adverse A
Volume sold		410,000		
	£'000	£'000	£'000	
Sales revenue		14,350		
Less costs:				
Direct materials		2,460		
Direct labour		1,640		
Overheads		4,010		
Operating profit		6,240		

Task 10

(a) **Choose the correct word from the pick list.**

The internal rate of return (IRR) is the discount rate that will result in a
[▼] net present value.

Picklist:

Positive
Negative
Zero

If the IRR of a project is [▼] than the organisation's cost of capital then
the project should be accepted.

Picklist:

Higher
Lower

IRR [▼] take into account the time value of money.

Picklist:

Does
Does not

(b) A project has the following budgeted costs and inflows.

Initial cost	(£350,000)
Inflow 1 year later	£150,000
Inflow 2 years' later	£75,000
Inflow 3 years' later	£95,000
Inflow 4 years' later	£90,000

**Calculate the payback period of the proposed project to the nearest whole
month.**

The payback period is [   ] year(s) and [   ] month(s).

(c) A project has achieved a net present value of £6,000. What does this indicate?

[ ] The project should be rejected

[ ] The project should be accepted

[ ] The project will make £6,000 profit

[ ] The project will generate £6,000 in cash over its life

BPP PRACTICE ASSESSMENT 2
COSTS AND REVENUES

ANSWERS

Costs and Revenues BPP practice assessment 2

Task 1

(a)

If costs are increasing, FIFO will give a higher profit than LIFO as issues, which form cost of sales, are at the earlier, LOWER prices.

The weighted average method FALLS SOMEWHERE IN BETWEEN THE PROFITS GIVEN BY FIFO AND LIFO.

In the long-term, over the life of the business, any such differences will DISAPPEAR

(b)

2,100

Buffer inventory = reorder level – (average usage × average lead time)

= 5,700 – (200 × 18)

= 2,100

(c) $EOQ = \sqrt{\dfrac{2cd}{h}}$

Task 2

(ii), (iii) and (iv) only

Statement (i) is not correct. A debit to materials with a corresponding credit to work in progress (WIP) indicates that direct materials returned from production were £45,000.

Statement (ii) is correct. Direct costs of production are 'collected' in the WIP account.

Statement (iii) is correct. Indirect costs of production or overhead are 'collected' in the overhead control account.

Statement (iv) is correct. The purchases of materials on credit are credited to the payables account and debited to the materials control account.

Task 3

(a)

		Direct wages £	Indirect wages £
Basic 35 hours per week at £10 per hour		350	
Overtime of 4 hours due to machine breakdown			
	Basic 4 hrs @ £10	40	
	Premium 4 hrs @ £5		20
Overtime of 2 hrs at the request of customer			
	Basic 2 hrs @£10	20	
	Premium 2 hrs @ £5	10	
Total		420	20

(b)

	£
750 units @ £2.50	1,875
250 units @ £2.88	720
75 units @ £3.35	251.25
	2,846.25

Task 4

	Total £	A £	B £	Stores £	Canteen £
Indirect wages	75,700	7,800	4,700	21,200	42,000
Rent	24,000	9,600	6,400	3,200	4,800
Buildings insurance	2,000	800	533	267	400
Power	6,400	2,880	1,920	320	1,280
Heat and light	4,000	1,600	1,066	534	800
Supervisor's wages	10,000	10,000	–	–	–
Machinery depreciation	3,200	1,493	1,280	160	267
Machinery insurance	2,200	1,027	880	110	183
Total	127,500	35,200	16,779	25,791	49,730
Canteen		29,009	16,577	4,144	(49,730)
				29,935	
Stores		17,961	11,974	(29,935)	
		82,170	45,330	–	–

Workings

Rent, buildings insurance and heat and light are apportioned on the basis of floor area – 12:8:4:6.

Power is apportioned using the percentages given.

Supervisor's wages are allocated directly to department A.

Machinery depreciation and insurance are apportioned on the basis of the net book value of the machinery – 140:120:15:25.

Canteen costs are apportioned according to the number of staff that use it – 70:40:10.

The stores costs are apportioned on the basis of the number of materials requisitions.

Task 5

(a) The machine hour absorption rate is £ [5] per hour.

Overhead absorption rate $= \dfrac{\text{Budgeted overheads}}{\text{Budgeted machine hours}}$

$= \dfrac{£85,000}{17,000}$

$= £5$

The overhead for the period was [under] absorbed by £ [4,250].

Overhead over-/(under)-absorbed $=$ Overhead absorbed $-$ Overhead incurred

$= (21,250 \times £5) - £110,500$

$= £(4,250)$

(b)

	Debit £	Credit £	No entry in this a/c £
Overhead control account		✓	
Work in progress account			✓
Statement of profit or loss	✓		

Under-absorbed overhead means that the overhead charged to production was too low and so there must be a debit to the statement of profit or loss.

(c) The absorption costing profit for the period for product M will be:

[✓]   higher

than the marginal costing profit. The difference between the two profit figures will be £ [6,000]

Difference in profit $=$ change in inventory level $\times$ fixed overhead per unit

$= (6,000 - 6,750) \times (£8 \times 1)$

$= £6,000$

The absorption costing profit will be higher because inventories have increased, and fixed overheads have been carried forward in inventory.

Task 6

Batches produced and sold	4,000	6,000	9,000
	£	£	£
Sales revenue	140,000	210,000	315,000
Variable costs:			
• Direct materials	22,000	33,000	49,500
• Direct labour	50,000	75,000	112,500
• Overheads	28,000	42,000	63,000
Semi-variable costs:	16,750	22,750	31,750
Total cost	116,750	172,750	256,750
Total profit	23,250	37,250	58,250
Profit per batch (to 2 decimal places)	5.81	6.21	6.47

Task 7

(a)

Toy	Elephant	Giraffe
	£	£
Selling price per toy (W1)	2.00	2.00
Less: Unit variable costs		
Direct materials (W2)	0.16	0.20
Direct labour (W3)	0.60	0.50
Variable overheads (W4)	0.04	0.08
Contribution per toy*	1.2	1.22
Profit volume ratio (%)**	60%	61%

* Contribution = Selling price – Variable costs
** Profit volume ratio = Contribution ÷ selling price × 100%

Workings

1 **Selling price per bottle**

$$\text{Selling price per toy} = \frac{\text{Total sales revenue}}{\text{Sales(toys)}}$$

$$\text{Elephant} = \frac{£2,500}{1,250} = £2 \text{ per toy}$$

$$\text{Giraffe} = \frac{£3,500}{1,750} = £2 \text{ per toy}$$

2 **Direct materials per toy**

$$\text{Direct materials per toy} = \frac{\text{Total direct material costs}}{\text{Production volume}}$$

$$\text{Elephant} = \frac{£200}{1,250} = £0.16 \text{ per toy}$$

$$\text{Giraffe} = \frac{£350}{1,750} = £0.20 \text{ per toy}$$

3 **Direct labour cost per toy**

$$\text{Direct labour cost per toy} = \frac{\text{Total direct labour costs}}{\text{Production volume}}$$

$$\text{Elephant} = \frac{£750}{1,250} = £0.60 \text{ per toy}$$

$$\text{Giraffe} = \frac{£875}{1,750} = £0.50 \text{ per toy}$$

4 **Variable overheads per toy**

$$\text{Variable overheads per toy} = \frac{\text{Total variable overhead costs}}{\text{Production volume}}$$

$$\text{Elephant} = \frac{£50}{1,250} = £0.04 \text{ per toy}$$

$$\text{Giraffe} = \frac{£140}{1,750} = £0.08 \text{ per toy}$$

(b) Breakeven point = Fixed costs/Contribution per unit

= £750/1.22

= 615 units (to the nearest unit)

(c) Margin of safety = Budgeted sales units – breakeven sales units

= 1,750 – 615

= 1,135

Task 8

(a)

Job EIL	£
Direct materials (3 kg × £5)	15.00
Direct labour (4 hours × £9)	36.00
Production overheads (4 hours × £8)*	<u>32.00</u>
Total production cost	83.00
20% profit (£83.00 × 0.2)	16.60
Selling price for the job	99.60

$$* \text{ OAR} = \frac{£240,000}{30,000} = £8 \text{ per labour hour}$$

(b)

	Debit	Credit
Process account		✓
Abnormal loss account	✓	

Task 9

	Flexed Budget	Actual	Variance	Favourable (F) or Adverse (A)
Volume sold	410,000	410,000		
	£'000	£'000	£'000	
Sales revenue	12,300	14,350	2,050	F
Less costs:				
Direct materials	2,255	2,460	205	A
Direct labour	1,845	1,640	205	F
Overheads	3,250	4,010	760	A
Operating profit	4,950	6,240	1,290	F

Task 10

(a) The internal rate of return (IRR) is the discount rate that will result in a ☐ zero ☐ net present value.

   If the IRR of a project is ☐ higher ☐ than the organisation's cost of capital then the project should be accepted.

   IRR ☐ does ☐ take into account the time value of money.

(b) The payback period is **3** years and **4** months.

(c) The project should be accepted.

   A net present value is the value of all future cash flows of a project discounted at a particular cost of capital. A positive value indicates the project should be accepted.

BPP PRACTICE ASSESSMENT 3
COSTS AND REVENUES

Time allowed: 2½ hours

Costs and Revenues BPP practice assessment 3

Task 1

The inventory record shown below for the ZIPPO for the month of June has only been fully completed for the first three weeks of the month. The EOQ for the ZIPPO is 392 kg.

(a) **Complete ALL entries in the inventory record for month and for the closing balance at the end of June, using the LIFO method of issuing inventory.**

   (Show the costs per kilogram (kg) in £s to 3 decimal places; and the total costs in whole £s).

Inventory record for the ZIPPO

Date	Receipts Quantity kg	Cost per kg (£)	Total cost (£)	Issues Quantity kg	Cost per kg (£)	Total cost (£)	Balance Quantity kg	Total cost (£)
Balance as at 22 June							500	625
24 June	392	1.305	512				892	1,137
26 June				400		522	492	615
28 June	392	1.310	514				884	1,129
30 June				200	1.310	262	684	867

(b) **Complete the sentence below.**

   Using the FIFO method, the issue of 400 kg to production on 26 June would have been valued at a total of

£ 500

Task 2

Drag and drop the correct entries into the Journal below to record the following FOUR accounting transactions:

1. Return of fibre optic cable from production to inventory
2. Receipt of fibre optic cable into inventory, paying immediately by BACS
3. Issue of fibre optic cable from inventory to production
4. Receipt of fibre optic cable into inventory, paying on credit

The drag and drop choices are:

*   Dr. Trade Payables' Control, Cr. Inventory
*   Dr. Bank, Cr. Inventory
*   Dr. Inventory, Cr. Trade Payables' Control
*   Dr. Inventory, Cr. Bank
*   Dr. Production, Cr. Inventory
*   Dr. Inventory, Cr. Production

	Drag and drop choice
Transaction 1	
Transaction 2	
Transaction 3	
Transaction 4	

Task 3

Below is a weekly timesheet for one of Avila Ltd's employees, who is paid as follows:

*   For a basic shift every day from Monday to Friday, the basic pay is £13 per hour.

*   For any overtime in excess of the basic hours, on any day from Monday to Friday – the extra hours are paid at time-and-a-quarter (basic pay plus an overtime premium equal to quarter of basic pay).

*   For any hours worked on Saturday or Sunday, the hours are paid at double time (basic pay plus an overtime premium equal to basic pay).

(a) **Complete the gaps in the table below to calculate the labour cost.**

Employee's weekly timesheet for week ending 7 June

	Hours	Total pay £
Basic pay (including basic hours for overtime)	30	
Mon-Fri overtime premium	4	
Sat – Sun overtime premium	9	
Total		

(b) Employees are also entitled to a bonus of 25% of basic hourly rate for every unit of production in excess of the monthly target. The target for last month was 450 units and employee A produced 490 units.

What was employee A's bonus payment for the month?

£ _____

(c) At the end of the month there was a total closing work-in-progress of 4,200 units which were 85% complete with regard to labour.

What are the equivalent units of production with regard to labour of the closing work-in-progress?

_____ units

Task 4

Tagus Ltd's budgeted overheads for the next financial year are:

	£	£
Depreciation of plant and equipment		750,500
Power for production machinery		1,875,000
Rent and rates		120,500
Light and heat		32,500
Indirect labour costs:		
Maintenance	115,000	
Stores	37,850	
General Administration	225,000	
Total indirect labour cost		377,850

The following information is also available:

Department	Net book value of plant and equipment	Production machinery power usage (KwH)	Floor space (square metres)	Number of employees
Production centres:				
Glass moulding	1,250,000	225,000		7
Glass extrusion	1,750,000	185,000		5
Support cost centres:				
Maintenance			10,000	4
Stores			12,000	5
General Administration			8,000	2
Total	3,000,000	410,000	30,000	23

Overheads are allocated or apportioned on the most appropriate basis. The total overheads of the support cost centres are then reapportioned to the two production centres using the direct method.

- 45% of the Maintenance cost centre's time is spent maintaining production machinery in the Glass moulding production centre, and the remainder in the Glass extrusion production centre.

- The Stores cost centre makes 35% of its issues to the Glass moulding production centre, and 65% to the Glass extrusion production centre.

- General Administration supports the two production centres equally.

- There is no reciprocal servicing between the three support cost centres.

Complete the table showing the apportionment and reapportionment of overheads to the two production centres:

	Basis of apportionment	Glass moulding £	Glass extrusion £	Maintenance £	Stores £	General Admin £	Totals £
Depreciation of plant and equipment	NBV of plant and equipment						
Power for production machinery	Production machinery power usage (KwH)						
Rent and rates	Floor space						
Light and heat	Floor space						
Indirect labour	Allocated						
Totals							
Reapportion Maintenance							
Reapportion Stores							
Reapportion General Admin							
Total overheads to production centres							

Task 5

Next quarter Tagus Ltd's budgeted overheads and activity levels are:

	Glass moulding	Glass extrusion
Budgeted overheads (£)	280,650	300,115
Budgeted direct labour hours	15,550	18,450
Budgeted machine hours	4,350	6,745

(a) **What would be the budgeted overhead absorption rate for each department, if this were set based on their both being heavily automated?**

☐ Glass moulding £65/hour, Glass extrusion £16/hour

☐ Glass moulding £18/hour, Glass extrusion £44/hour

☐ Glass moulding £65/hour, Glass extrusion £44/hour

☐ Glass moulding £18/hour, Glass extrusion £16/hour

(b) **What would be the budgeted overhead absorption rate for each department, if this were set based on their both being labour intensive?**

☐ Glass moulding £65/hour, Glass extrusion £16/hour

☐ Glass moulding £18/hour, Glass extrusion £44/hour

☐ Glass moulding £65/hour, Glass extrusion £44/hour

☐ Glass moulding £18/hour, Glass extrusion £16/hour

Additional data

At the end of the quarter actual overheads incurred were found to be:

	Glass moulding	Glass extrusion
Actual overheads (£)	315,906	285,550

(c) **Assuming that exactly the same amount of overheads was absorbed as budgeted, what were the budgeted under- or over-absorptions in the quarter?**

☐ Glass moulding over-absorbed £35,256, Glass extrusion over-absorbed £14,565

☐ Glass moulding over-absorbed £35,256, Glass extrusion under-absorbed £14,565

☐ Glass moulding under-absorbed £35,256, Glass extrusion under-absorbed £14,565

☐ Glass moulding under-absorbed £35,256, Glass extrusion over-absorbed £14,565

Task 6

Lisboa Ltd has prepared a forecast for the next quarter for one of its small plastic components, ZEST. This component is produced in batches and the forecast is based on selling and producing 2,400 batches.

One of the customers of Lisboa Ltd has indicated that it may be significantly increasing its order level for component ZEST for the next quarter and it appears that activity levels of 3,500 batches and 4,000 batches are feasible.

The semi-variable costs should be calculated using the high-low method. If 6,000 batches are sold the total semi-variable cost will be £14,754, and there is a constant unit variable cost up to this volume.

Complete the table below and calculate the estimated profit per batch of ZEST at the different activity levels:

Batches produced and sold	2,400	3,500	4,000
	£	£	£
Sales revenue	45,500		
Variable costs:			
• Direct materials	11,250		
• Direct labour	10,850		
• Overheads	6,825		
Semi-variable costs:	8,400		
• Variable element			
• Fixed element			
Total cost	37,325		
Total profit	8,175		
Profit per batch (to 2 decimal places)	3.41		

Task 7

Product TEST has a selling price of £32 per unit with a total variable cost of £24 per unit. Avignon Ltd estimates that the fixed costs per quarter associated with this product are £43,000.

(a) **Calculate the budgeted breakeven, in units, for product TEST.**

	units

(b) **Calculate the budgeted breakeven, in £s, for product TEST.**

£	

(c) **Complete the table below to show the budgeted margin of safety in units and the margin of safety percentage if Avignon Ltd sells 5,500 units or 7,000 units of product TEST:**

Units of TEST sold	5,500	7,000
	£	£
Margin of safety (units)		
Margin of safety percentage		

(d) **If Avignon Ltd wishes to make a profit of £35,000, how many units of TEST must it sell?**

	units

(e) **If Avignon Ltd decreases the selling price of TEST by 10p what will be the impact on the breakeven point and the margin of safety, assuming no change in the number of units sold?**

- ☐ The breakeven point will decrease and the margin of safety will increase.
- ☐ The breakeven point will stay the same but the margin of safety will decrease.
- ☐ The breakeven point will increase and the margin of safety will decrease.
- ☐ The breakeven point will increase and the margin of safety stay the same.

Task 8

The Glass moulding department of Seville Ltd uses process costing for some of its products.

The process account for June for one particular process has been partly completed but the following information is also relevant:

Two employees worked on this process during June. Each employee worked 35 hours per week for 4 weeks and was paid £14 per hour.

Overheads are absorbed on the basis of £17 per labour hour.

Seville Ltd expects a normal loss of 7.5% during this process, which it then sells for scrap at 50p per kg.

(a) **Complete the process account below for June:**

Description	Kg	Unit cost £	Total cost £	Description	Kg	Unit cost £	Total cost £
Material G4	700	1.30		Normal loss		0.50	
Material G3	500	1.40		Output			
Material G9	500	1.10					
Labour							
Overheads							

(b) **Identify the correct journal entries for an abnormal gain:**

	Debit	Credit
Process account		
Abnormal gain account		

Task 9

Bilbao Ltd has the following original budget and actual performance for product SCOOT for the year ending 30 June:

	Budget	Actual
Volume sold	50,000	44,000
	£'000	£'000
Sales revenue	1,750	1,496
Less costs:		
Direct materials	150	130
Direct labour	200	280
Overheads	950	928
Operating profit	450	158

Both direct materials and direct labour are variable costs, but the overheads are fixed.

Complete the table below to show a flexed budget and the resulting variances against this budget for the year. Show the actual variance amount for sales, each cost, and operating profit, in the column headed 'Variance' and indicate whether this is Favourable or Adverse by entering F or A in the final column. If neither F nor A enter 0.

	Flexed Budget	Actual	Variance	Favourable F or Adverse A
Volume sold		44,000		
	£'000	£'000	£'000	
Sales revenue		1,496		
Less costs:				
Direct materials		130		
Direct labour		280		
Overheads		928		
Operating profit		158		

Task 10

One of the moulding machines in the Glass extrusion department is nearing the end of its useful life and Bilbao Ltd is considering purchasing a replacement machine.

Estimates have been made for the initial capital cost, sales income and operating costs of the replacement machine, which is expected to have a useful life of three years:

	Year 0 £'000	Year 1 £'000	Year 2 £'000	Year 3 £'000
Capital expenditure	900			
Other cash flows:				
Sales income		540	660	780
Operating costs		300	310	320

The company appraises capital investment projects using a 12% cost of capital.

(a) **Complete the table below and calculate the net present value of the proposed replacement machine (to the nearest £'000):**

	Year 0 £'000	Year 1 £'000	Year 2 £'000	Year 3 £'000
Capital expenditure				
Sales income				
Operating costs				
Net cash flows				
PV factors	1.0000	0.8929	0.7972	0.7118
Discounted cash flows				
Net present value				

The net present value is [　　　　▼].

Picklist:

Positive
Negative

(b) **Calculate the payback period of the proposed replacement machine to the nearest whole month.**

The payback period is [   ] year(s) and [   ] month(s).

BPP PRACTICE ASSESSMENT 3
COSTS AND REVENUES

ANSWERS

Costs and Revenues BPP practice assessment 3

Task 1

(a)

Date	Receipts			Issues			Balance	
	Quantity kg	Cost per kg (£)	Total cost (£)	Quantity kg	Cost per kg (£)	Total cost (£)	Quantity kg	Total cost (£)
Balance as at 22 June							500	625
24 June	392	1.305	512				892	1,137
26 June				400	1.305	522	492	615
28 June	392	1.310	514				884	1,129
30 June				200	1.310	262	684	867

(b)   £500.00

£625 / 500kg = £1.25 per kg

£1.25 per kg × 400kg = £500.00

··

Task 2

	Drag and drop choice
Transaction 1	Dr. Inventory, Cr. Production
Transaction 2	Dr. Inventory, Cr. Bank
Transaction 3	Dr. Production, Cr. Inventory
Transaction 4	Dr. Inventory, Cr. Trade payables' Control

··

Task 3

(a) **Employee's weekly timesheet for week ending 7 July**

	Hours	Total pay £
Basic pay (including basic hours for overtime)	30	390
Mon-Fri overtime premium	4	13
Sat – Sun overtime premium	9	117
Total		520

(b) | £130 |

£13 × 25% = £3.25 per unit

40 extra units × £3.25 = £130

(c) | 3,570 | units

4,200 units × 85% = 3,570 units

Task 4

	Basis of apportionment	Glass moulding £	Glass extrusion £	Maintenance £	Stores £	General Admin £	Totals £
Depreciation of plant and equipment	NBV of plant and equipment	312,708	437,792				750,500
Power for production machinery	Production machinery power usage (KwH)	1,028,963	846,037				1,875,000
Rent and rates	Floor space			40,167	48,200	32,133	120,500
Light and heat	Floor space			10,833	13,000	8,667	32,500
Indirect labour	Allocated			115,000	37,850	225,000	377,850
Totals		1,341,671	1,283,829	166,000	99,050	265,800	3,156,350
Reapportion Maintenance		74,700	91,300	(166,000)			
Reapportion Stores		34,668	64,382		(99,050)		
Reapportion General Admin		132,900	132,900			(265,800)	
Total overheads to production centres		1,583,939	1,572,411				3,156,350

Task 5

(a) The correct answer is Glass moulding £65/hour, Glass extrusion £44/hour

(b) The correct answer is Glass moulding £18/hour, Glass extrusion £16/hour

(c) The correct answer is Glass moulding under-absorbed £35,256, Glass extrusion over-absorbed £14,565

Task 6

Batches produced and sold	2,400	3,500	4,000
	£	£	£
Sales revenue	45,500	66,354	75,833
Variable costs:			
• Direct materials	11,250	16,406	18,750
• Direct labour	10,850	15,823	18,083
• Overheads	6,825	9,953	11,375
Semi-variable costs:	8,400		
• Variable element		6,178	7,060
• Fixed element		4,164	4,164
Total cost	37,325	52,524	59,432
Total profit	8,175	13,830	16,401
Profit per batch (to 2 decimal places)	3.41	3.95	4.10

Task 7

(a) | 5,375 units |

(b) | £172,000 |

(c)

Units of TEST sold	5,500	7,000
	£	£
Margin of safety (units)	125	1,625
Margin of safety percentage	2%	23%

(d) | 9,750 units |

(e) The correct answer is The breakeven point will increase and the margin of safety will decrease.

Task 8

(a)

Description	Kg	Unit cost £	Total cost £	Description	Kg	Unit cost £	Total cost £
Material G4	700	1.30	910	Normal loss	128	0.50	64
Material G3	500	1.40	700	Output	1,572	6.85	10,776
Material G9	500	1.10	550				
Labour			3,920				
Overheads			4,760				
	1,700		10,840		1,700		10,840

(b)

	Debit	Credit
Process account	✓	
Abnormal gain account		✓

Task 9

	Flexed Budget	Actual	Variance	Favourable F or Adverse A
Volume sold	44,000	44,000		
	£'000	£'000	£'000	
Sales revenue	1,540	1,496	44	A
Less costs:				
Direct materials	132	130	2	F
Direct labour	176	280	104	A
Overheads	950	928	22	F
Operating profit	282	158	124	A

Task 10

(a)

	Year 0 £'000	Year 1 £'000	Year 2 £'000	Year 3 £'000
Capital expenditure	(900)			
Sales income		540	660	780
Operating costs		(300)	(310)	(320)
Net cash flows	(900)	240	350	460
PV factors	1.0000	0.8929	0.7972	0.7118
Discounted cash flows	(900)	214	279	327
Net present value	(80)			

The net present value is **negative**.

(b)   The payback period is **2** years and **8** months.

BPP PRACTICE ASSESSMENT 4
COSTS AND REVENUES

Time allowed: 2½ hours

Costs and Revenues BPP practice assessment 4

Task 1

The following information is available for telephone cable held by Beppo Ltd:

- Annual demand 78,125 kilograms
- Annual holding cost per kilogram £1.25
- Fixed ordering cost £2.50

(a) **Calculate the Economic Order Quantity (EOQ) for telephone cable.**

The inventory record shown below for TELEPHONE CABLE for the month of May has only been fully completed for the first three weeks of the month.

(b) **Complete the entries in the inventory record for the two receipts on 24 and 28 May that were ordered using the EOQ method.**

(c) **Complete ALL entries in the inventory record for the two issues in the month and for the closing balance at the end of May, using the FIFO method of issuing inventory.**

(Show the costs per kilogram (kg) in £s to 3 decimal places; and the total costs in whole £s).

Inventory record for TELEPHONE CABLE

Date	Receipts			Issues			Balance	
	Quantity kg	Cost per kg (£)	Total cost (£)	Quantity kg	Cost per kg (£)	Total cost (£)	Quantity kg	Total cost (£)
Balance as at 22 May							250	625
24 May		2.30						
26 May				275				
28 May		2.50						
31 May				350				

Task 2

A company had the following transactions during March 20X1:

1.	Spend on production overheads	£3,150
2.	Direct labour (350 hrs)	£3,850
3.	Indirect labour – production salaries	£1,350
4.	Indirect labour – admin salaries	£1,100
5.	Depreciation of factory plant and machinery	£120
6.	Depreciation of office equipment	£50
7.	Production overheads absorbed per direct labour hour	£12.50

(a) **Complete the following journals relating to the production overhead account for March 20X1:**

DR	Production overhead control account	£
CR	Wages and salaries control account	£
DR	Production overhead control account	£
CR	Depreciation account	£
DR	Production overhead control account	£
CR	Bank	£
DR	WIP Account	£
CR	Production overhead control account	£

(b) **What is the under or over absorption of overheads during March 20X1?**

£ [   ]   [▼]

Picklist:

Under
Over

Task 3

BYC Ltd is a busy telesales and internet sales company based in Europe. Employees at BYC work 40 core hours per week based on 8 hours per day. Payment for core hours, overtime and bonuses are as follows:

- Core hours are paid at £10.60 per hour.

- A premium of half the hourly rate is paid for weekday overtime.

- Any calls/requests handled beyond 500 in any one week will attract a bonus per call/request of £0.30.

- An additional weekly bonus will be paid if a worker handles more than 1,000 calls in any one week. This bonus is £1,000.

The hours worked and calls/requests handled for one employee, Bill Raynet, for week 29 were as follows:

Bill Raynet	Employee number: 567	Week 29
	Hours worked	Calls/requests handled
Monday	9	197
Tuesday	8	193
Wednesday	10	464
Thursday	8	167
Friday	9	245

Using the information provided:

(a) **Calculate the total pay for Bill Raynet in week 29 (to 2 decimal places).**

£ [ ]

(b) **How much of Bill's pay will be allocated to indirect labour costs?**

(State your answer to the nearest whole £.)

£ [ ]

(c) **If the one-off bonus of £1,000 was scrapped and replaced by an overall increase in the core hourly rate of 5%, what would Bill's total pay be for week 29? (to 2 decimal places).**

£ ☐

(d) **With the increase in the core pay of 5%, how much of Bill's pay will be allocated to direct labour costs in week 29? (State your answer to the nearest whole £.)**

£ ☐

Task 4

Beppo Ltd's budgeted overheads for the next financial year are:

	£	£
Depreciation of plant and equipment		1,005,188
Power for production machinery		893,750
Rent and rates		130,625
Light and heat		28,875
Indirect labour costs:		
Maintenance	126,438	
Stores	45,063	
General Administration	300,125	
Total indirect labour cost		471,626

The following information is also available:

Department	Net book value of plant and equipment	Production machinery power usage (KwH)	Floor space (square metres)	Number of employees
Production centres:				
Wire plaiting	7,000,000	2,681,250		12
Wire extrusion	3,000,000	1,787,500		10
Support cost centres:				
Maintenance			17,500	4
Stores			10,500	2
General Administration			7,000	3
Total	10,000,000	4,468,750	35,000	31

Overheads are allocated or apportioned on the most appropriate basis. The total overheads of the support cost centres are then reapportioned to the two production centres using the direct method.

- 55% of the Maintenance cost centre's time is spent maintaining production machinery in the Wire plaiting production centre, and the remainder in the Wire extrusion production centre.

- The Stores cost centre makes 70% of its issues to the Wire plaiting production centre, and 30% to the Wire extrusion production centre.

- General Administration supports the two production centres equally.

- There is no reciprocal servicing between the three support cost centres.

Complete the table showing the apportionment and reapportionment of overheads to the two production centres:

	Basis of apportionment	Wire plaiting £	Wire extrusion £	Maintenance £	Stores £	General Admin £	Totals £
Depreciation of plant and equipment	NBV of plant and equipment						
Power for production machinery	Production machinery power usage (KwH)						
Rent and rates	Floor space						
Light and heat	Floor space						
Indirect labour	Allocated						
Totals							
Reapportion Maintenance							
Reapportion Stores							
Reapportion General Admin							
Total overheads to production centres							

Task 5

Next quarter Beppo Ltd's budgeted overheads and activity levels are:

	Wire plaiting	Wire extrusion
Budgeted overheads (£)	407,495	222,750
Budgeted direct labour hours	25,750	24,750
Budgeted machine hours	11,145	8,500

(a) **What would be the budgeted overhead absorption rate for each department, if this were set based on their both being heavily automated?**

☐ Wire plaiting £16/hour, Wire extrusion £9/hour

☐ Wire plaiting £16/hour, Wire extrusion £26/hour

☐ Wire plaiting £37/hour, Wire extrusion £9/hour

☐ Wire plaiting £37/hour, Wire extrusion £26/hour

(b) **What would be the budgeted overhead absorption rate for each department, if this were set based on their both being labour intensive?**

☐ Wire plaiting £16/hour, Wire extrusion £9/hour

☐ Wire plaiting £16/hour, Wire extrusion £26/hour

☐ Wire plaiting £37/hour, Wire extrusion £9/hour

☐ Wire plaiting £37/hour, Wire extrusion £26/hour

Additional data

At the end of the quarter actual overheads incurred were found to be:

	Wire plaiting	Wire extrusion
Actual overheads (£)	425,350	247,625

(c) **Assuming that exactly the same amount of overheads was absorbed as budgeted, what were the budgeted under- or over-absorptions in the quarter?**

☐ Wire plaiting over-absorbed £17,855, Wire extrusion over-absorbed £24,875

☐ Wire plaiting over-absorbed £17,855, Wire extrusion under-absorbed £24,875

☐ Wire plaiting under-absorbed £17,855, Wire extrusion under-absorbed £24,875

☐ Wire plaiting under-absorbed £17,855, Wire extrusion over-absorbed £24,875

Task 6

ABC Ltd is in the process of setting production levels for the coming year. The following information is available:

1   Production levels can be either 10,000, 12,000, 14,000 or 16,000 units.

2   All units produced can be sold at a price of £21 per unit.

3   Direct material costs are £6 per unit.

4   Direct labour is £8 per unit up to a production level of 12,000 units. Above this level of production additional supervisors will be required increasing the cost to £9 per unit

5   The machine overheads are semi-variable, dependent on the number of production machines required. The overheads per machine are £11,000. Three machines are required up to a production level of 14,000 units. A fourth machine will be required to produce 16,000 units.

6   General overheads should be calculated using the high-low method. If 10,000 units are produced, the total general overheads will be £18,000. If 16,000 units are produced, the total general overheads will increase to £22,500. (The variable overhead remains constant between these two different production levels.)

(a)   **Calculate the profit achieved at each production level.**

(b)   **State the optimum production level.**

(a)   **Complete the following table:**

	10,000 units	12,000 units	14,000 units	16,000 units
Sales Revenue				
Direct materials				
Direct labour				
Machine overheads				
General overheads				
Total costs				
Profit				

(b)   **Optimum production level:**

Units

Task 7

XYZ limited has two KPIs (key performance indicators) which are important in setting price and production levels for product P.

The KPIs are:

1 To maximise market share achieved by product P

2 To maximise contribution generated by product P

The demand for product P for the next year at various selling prices is forecast to be:

Sales price (£)	Demand
15	13,000
16	12,500
17	12,000
18	11,000
19	10,000
20	8,000

The production costs for product P for next year are:	
Fixed overheads	£80,000
Direct materials per unit	£3.50
Direct labour per unit	£5.50

XYZ Ltd's strategy is to maximise market share by selling at as low a price as possible. The exact levels of demand are still uncertain so XYZ Ltd has set a break-even volume of 10,000 units.

(a) **If the break-even volume (units) is set at 10,000, what selling price should be set?**

☐ £19

☐ £17

☐ £15

☐ £13

(b) **What will be the expected profit earned by XYZ Ltd for product P at this selling price?**

£ _____

(c) **What is the forecast margin of safety for product P at this selling price? Express your answer as a percentage of XYZ Ltd's break-even volume of 10,000 units (to 1 decimal place).**

	%

(d) **What is the Profit Volume Ratio for XYZ Ltd at the selling price identified in part (a)?**

(Provide your answer to 1 decimal place.)

	%

Task 8

Product W123 has the following estimated costs per unit.

Product W123	£ per unit
Direct materials	16.50
Direct labour	21.60
Variable overheads	4.50
Fixed manufacturing overheads	6.90
Fixed administration, selling and distribution costs	5.10
Total costs	54.60

(a) **What is the full absorption cost of one unit of Em?**

£ [   ]

(b) **What is an equivalent unit?**

☐ A unit of output which is identical to all others manufactured in the same process

☐ Notional whole units used to represent uncompleted work

☐ A unit of product in relation to which costs are ascertained

☐ The amount of work achievable, at standard efficiency levels, in an hour

(c) Process B had no opening or closing inventory. 64,200 kg were input into the process at a value of £130,000. The normal loss is 10% of input. The output was 57,500 kg.

Calculate the abnormal loss or gain in kg.

[   ] kg [▼]

Picklist:

Loss

Gain

(d) Sometimes materials are lost during processing and the materials may be scrapped; sometimes scrap may have a value. **If this is the case, the accounting treatment for the scrap value of normal loss is:**

Debit [▼] account

Credit [▼] account

Picklist:

Scrap
Process

Task 9

One Ltd set a budget for December 20X1 based on sales of 6,000 units. However, during the year actual sales were only 5,800 units. The budget together with actual sales and costs is shown below:

	Budget	Actual
Volume sold	6,000	5,800
	£	£
Sales revenue	114,000	109,250
Less costs:		
Material A	33,000	33,450
Material B	21,000	29,150
Direct labour	22,500	20,500
Overheads – Fixed	17,500	17,600
Overheads – Variable	10,500	9,900
Profit	9,500	(1,350)

All materials and direct labour costs are variable costs.

(a) **Calculate the flexed budget and the variances between the flexed budget and actual results, for Dec 20X1.**

(b) **Indicate whether a variance is favourable or adverse using letters F or A.**

	Flexed Budget	Actual	Variances	F/A
Volume sold	5,800	5,800		
	£	£	£	
Sales Revenue		109,250		
Material A		33,450		
Material B		29,150		
Direct labour		20,500		
Overheads – fixed		17,600		
Overheads – variable		9,900		
Profit		(1,350)		

(c) **What is the primary reason for One Ltd making a loss during December 20X1, when it had originally budgeted to make a profit?**

☐ An increase in fixed overheads

☐ Sales being less than budgeted

☐ An increase in time taken to manufacture each unit

☐ An increase in the use and/or the cost of materials

Task 10

A company is considering buying new production machinery. The cost and depreciation for the machinery are as follows:

Cost		£150,000
Depreciation	Year 1	£15,000
	Year 2	£15,000
	Year 3	£15,000
Expected sales value	Year 3	£100,000
Expected loss on disposal	Year 3	£5,000

The machinery is forecast to give the following cost savings:

Net cash savings	Year 1	£28,000
	Year 2	£30,000
	Year 3	£32,000

The company appraises projects using a cost of capital of 11%.

PV factors
1.0000
0.9009
0.8116
0.7312

(a) **On the assumption that the company will sell the machinery for the expected value at the end of year 3, what is the net present value (NPV) of the project?**

(Use the – sign to show a negative number)

£ _____

(b) **Should the company accept or reject the opportunity to produce this piece of machinery?**

_____ ▼

Picklist:

Accept
Reject

(c) **How much of a profit or loss will this piece of machinery contribute to the company over the three years?**

£	▼

Picklist:

Profit
Loss

(d) **What is the main reason for the difference between the answers to (b) and (c)?**

☐ The depreciation charged each year is not sufficient to cover the loss on the sale of the machine.

☐ The contribution towards profit does not take into account the time value of money.

☐ The sale proceeds for the machine in three years' time cannot be known with certainty.

☐ The company may be able to buy a second hand machine for less than £150,000.

BPP PRACTICE ASSESSMENT 4
COSTS AND REVENUES

ANSWERS

Costs and Revenues BPP practice assessment 4

Task 1

(a) **The EOQ is 559 kg =** $\sqrt{\dfrac{2 \times 78{,}125 \times 2.5}{1.25}}$

(b) **and** (c) **Inventory record card**

Date	Receipts			Issues			Balance	
	Quantity kg	Cost per kg (£)	Total cost (£)	Quantity kg	Cost per kg (£)	Total cost (£)	Quantity kg	Total cost (£)
Balance as at 22 May							250	625
24 May	559	2.30	1,286				809	1,911
26 May				275	2.50/2.30	683	534	1,228
28 May	559	2.50	1,398				1,093	2,626
31 May				350	2.30	805	743	1,821

Task 2

(a) Journals relating to the production overhead account for March 20X1:

DR	Production overhead control account	£ 1,350
CR	Wages and salaries control account	£ 1,350
DR	Production overhead control account	£ 120
CR	Depreciation account	£ 120
DR	Production overhead control account	£ 3,150
CR	Bank	£ 3,150
DR	WIP Account (350 × 12.50)	£ 4,375
CR	Production overhead control account	£ 4,375

(b) Under absorption of overheads during March 20X1

(1350 + 120 + 3150) – 4375 = 245

£ 245		Under

Task 3

	Hours worked	Calls/requests handled	Pay at core rate	Overtime hrs	Premium £	Total £
Monday	9	197	95.40	1	5.30	100.70
Tuesday	8	193	84.80	0	0.00	84.80
Wednesday	10	464	106.00	2	10.60	116.60
Thursday	8	167	84.80	0	0.00	84.80
Friday	9	245	95.40	1	5.30	100.70
Total	44	1,266	466.40		21.20	487.60

Requests handled over 500	766	Bonus payment for over 1,000 calls/requests	£1,000
Bonus payment	**229.80**		

(a) **Total pay** for Bill in week 29

Total pay (487.60) + Bonus over 500 (229.80) + Bonus over 1,000 (1,000)

£1,717.40

(b) Pay allocated to **indirect labour** costs

Bonus + premium payments = 229.80 + 1,000 + 21.20

£1,251

(c) Bill's **total pay** for week 29 if the £1,000 bonus was scrapped:

£741.79	Or £741.78 depending on rounding

Core rate = 11.13 (10.60 × 1.05)

	Hours worked	Calls/requests handled	Pay at core rate	Overtime hrs	Premium £	Total £
Monday	9	197	100.17	1	5.57	105.74
Tuesday	8	193	89.04	0	0.00	89.04
Wednesday	10	464	111.30	2	11.13	122.43
Thursday	8	167	89.04	0	0.00	89.04
Friday	9	245	100.17	1	5.57	105.74
Total	44	1,266	**489.72**		**22.27**	**511.99**

Requests handled over 500	
	766
Payment	**229.80**

Total pay = 511.99 + 229.80 = £741.79

(d) Pay allocated to **direct labour** costs in week 29 if the £1,000 bonus was scrapped:

£490

Task 4

	Basis of apportionment	Wire plaiting £	Wire extrusion £	Maintenance £	Stores £	General Admin £	Totals £
Depreciation of plant and equipment	NBV of plant and equipment	703,632	301,556				1,005,188
Power for production machinery	Production machinery power usage (KwH)	536,250	357,500				893,750
Rent and rates	Floor space			65,312	39,188	26,125	130,625
Light and heat	Floor space			14,438	8,662	5,775	28,875
Indirect labour	Allocated			126,438	45,063	300,125	471,626
Totals		1,239,882	659,056	206,188	92,913	332,025	2,530,064
Reapportion Maintenance		113,403	92,785	(206,188)			
Reapportion Stores		65,039	27,874		(92,913)		
Reapportion General Admin		166,012	166,013			(332,025)	
Total overheads to production centres		1,584,336	945,728				2,530,064

Task 5

(a) The correct answer is Wire plaiting £37/hour, Wire extrusion £26/hour

(b) The correct answer is Wire plaiting £16/hour, Wire extrusion £9/hour

(c) The correct answer is Wire plaiting under-absorbed £17,855, Wire extrusion under-absorbed £24,875

Task 6

(a)

	10,000 units	12,000 units	14,000 units	16,000 units
Sales Revenue	210,000	252,000	294,000	336,000
Direct materials	60,000	72,000	84,000	96,000
Direct labour	80,000	96,000	126,000	144,000
Machine overheads	33,000	33,000	33,000	44,000
General overheads	18,000	19,500	21,000	22,500
Total costs	191,000	220,500	264,000	306,500
Profit	19,000	31,500	30,000	29,500

(b)   Optimum production level

12,000   Units

....

Task 7

(a)   The correct answer is £17.

Sales price (£)	Contribution (£)	Break-even units
15	6	13,333
16	7	11,429
17	**8**	**10,000**
18	9	8,889
19	10	8,000
20	11	7,273

(b)   The expected profit earned

	£
Sales (£17 × 12,000)	204,000
Direct materials (£3.50 × 12,000)	(42,000)
Direct labour (£5.50 × 12,000)	(66,000)
Fixed overheads	(80,000)
Profit	16,000

(c) Working (2,000/12,000) × 100 = 16.7%

(d) Contribution/sales = (£8/£17) × 100 = 47.1%

Task 8

(a) | **£49.50** |

£54.60 – £5.10 = £49.50

(b) **Notional whole units used to represent uncompleted work**

An equivalent unit calculation is used in process costing to value any **incomplete units** within **work in progress and losses**.

The first option describes the output from any process, where all completed units are **identical**.

The third describes a cost unit, and the final option describes a **standard hour**.

(c) 280 kg abnormal loss

Materials input = 64,200 kg so normal loss = 64,200 × 10% = 6,420 and expected output = 64,200 kg – 6,420 kg = 57,780 kg.

Actual output was 57,500 kg and so there was an abnormal loss of 57,780 kg – 57,500 kg = 280 kg

(d) Debit | scrap | account

Credit | process | account

Task 9

(a) + (b)

	Flexed Budget	Actual	Variances	F/A
Volume sold	5,800	5,800		
	£	£	£	
Sales Revenue	110,200	109,250	950	A
Material A	31,900	33,450	1,550	A
Material B	20,300	29,150	8,850	A
Direct labour	21,750	20,500	1,250	F
Overheads – fixed	17,500	17,600	100	A
Overheads – variable	10,150	9,900	250	F
Profit	8,600	(1,350)	9,950	A

(c) The answer is An increase in the use and/or the cost of materials

....

Task 10

(a) The net present value (NPV) of the project:

Time	Cash costs	Cash inflows	Net cash flows	PV factors	Discounted cash flows
0	(150,000)		(150,000)	1.0000	(150,000)
1		28,000	28,000	0.9009	25,225
2		30,000	30,000	0.8116	24,348
3		132,000	132,000	0.7312	96,518
			Net present value		(3,909)

NPV £-3,909

(b) Should the company accept or reject the opportunity to produce this piece of machinery?

Reject

(c) The profit is calculated:

Year 1	28,000 – 15,000 (savings less depreciation)	£13,000
Year 2	30,000 – 15,000 (savings less depreciation)	£15,000
Year 3	32,000 – 15,000 – 5,000 (savings less depreciation less loss on disposal)	£12,000
Total		£40,000

£ 40,000	Profit

(d) The correct answer is The contribution towards profit does not take into account the time value of money.